STANDING BY
AND
MAKING DO:
Women of Wartime Los Alamos

Jane S. Wilson and Charlotte Serber, Editors

D0556077

The Los Alamos Historical Society
Los Alamos, New Mexico
1988

Library of Congress Cataloging-in-Publication Data

Standing by and making do.

  1. Atomic bomb—History. 2. Manhattan Project (U.S.)—History.
3. Wives—New Mexico—Los Alamos—Effect of husband's employ-
ment on—History.
I. Wilson, Jane, 1916– . II. Serber, Charlotte.
QC773.AlS82 1988   355.8'25119'09   88-26761
ISBN 0-941232-08-5 (pbk.)

Printed in the United States of America

CONTENTS

FOREWORD

By 1945 the United States Manhattan Project had designed, assembled, and tested the first atomic weapons. After two of these weapons were used on Japan, the long years of World War II were over. The nerve center of the Manhattan Project was located in Los Alamos, a secret, isolated, 7200-foot-high, built-from-scratch village in the Jemez Mountains of north-central New Mexico. Here, Robert Oppenheimer, the scientific director of the Project, had assembled scientists from the United States and Europe. Supporting the scientific endeavor were men and women of the US Army. The village was named after the Los Alamos Ranch School. Before 1943, the school and a few scattered ranchers were the only occupants of the area. The US Army took over the school and ranches and built laboratories, test facilities, and rudimentary living quarters.

Starting in late 1943, families of the scientists and service personnel moved to the remote and heavily guarded village. Their nearest neighbors were 15 to 20 miles away at the Indian pueblos of San Ildefonso and Santa Clara. The lights of Santa Fe could be seen 35 miles to the east, across the Rio Grande valley. Getting permission and transportation to visit Santa Fe was not easily arranged.

With the successful conclusion of the Manhattan Project and the end of World War II, many of the Project people at Los Alamos began to think of returning to peacetime pursuits. They also began to think of what they had accomplished and its possible historical significance.

Others, including a group of women who had been living in Los Alamos, had similar thoughts. In January of 1946, when Robert Marshak received a publisher's request for a human-interest story about Los Alamos, he handed it to his wife, Ruth. By mid-February, she had organized the group, drawn up a book plan, assigned subjects, and allotted tasks. Each woman wrote one chapter. Jane Wilson (with help from Charlotte Serber) compiled the chapters, edited the whole manuscript, and wrote the introduction. Although many of these women had already left Los Alamos by 1946, Ruth Marshak assured the publisher in her answer to the initial request, "We carefully planned our program before breaking up."

However, that publisher—and then another—rejected the book. Thirty years later Jane Wilson gave the manuscript to the Los Alamos Historical Museum, where for a decade it intrigued readers in the Museum's archives. In 1987, the Los Alamos Historical Society's Publications Committee reviewed manuscripts from the archival collection and chose the women's stories for publication. The Historical Society funded the project.

The Los Alamos Historical Society is indebted to many persons for their help in publishing this, its ninth book. The Society owes special thanks to original authors Jean Bacher, Shirley B. Barnett, Kathleen Mark, Ruth Marshak, Alice Kimball Smith, and Jane S. Wilson; we also owe thanks to Kevin McKibbin, Paul Masters, and Robert Serber, surviving relatives of Dorothy McKibbin, Charlie Masters, and Charlotte Serber, for their cooperation in this project. For the Historical Society, Publications Committee members Lore Watt, Janice Baker, Kitty Fluharty, Betty Leffler, and I selected the manuscript. Hedy Dunn, Los Alamos Historical Museum director, and Bill Jack Rodgers of the Los Alamos National Laboratory provided illustrations. Editors Baker and Leffler prepared the manuscript for publication. With the cooperation of the six women still living and relatives of those who have died, they updated the brief biographies and edited the 1946 manuscript lightly to identify people, places, and organizations not immediately recognizable to readers in the 1980s, but with attention to preserving the women's wartime attitudes and phraseology.

In this book, at long last, are published the accounts these women wrote in 1946. They are not retrospective thoughts written forty years later: instead, they are essentially real-time accounts of their experiences in Los Alamos during the war years. As will be noted in their

individual biographies, many of the women continued their interest
in writing.

Luther L. Lyon
Los Alamos Historical Society
1988

Note: Luther Lyon died in April of 1988. As a member of our committee
and then as Historical Society president, he was the moving force
behind this publication. We dedicate our work on this book to his
memory.

Publications Committee, Los Alamos Historical Society
Lore Watt, Chairman
Janice Baker
Kitty Fluharty
Betty Leffler

STANDING BY
AND
MAKING DO:
Women of Wartime Los Alamos

Jane S. Wilson and Charlotte Serber, Editors

To our husbands
and to all the men who made the atomic bomb a reality
this book is affectionately dedicated.

INTRODUCTION

July 16, 1945

During the long hours, Sawyer's Hill, a ski slope in the Jemez Mountains of New Mexico, was a good place to stand. From it one faced south, and the view was unobstructed. Some women could watch from the porches of the houses where they lived. Of course there were those who overslept and others who were unaware and so did not keep vigil at all.

The test was scheduled for four in the morning. The air seemed empty and bitter cold, although it was July. It was very dark and only when one's eyes became accustomed to the night could one make out the silhouettes of the pine trees against the starless sky.

Four o'clock. Nothing was happening. Perhaps something was amiss down there in the desert where one's husband stood with the other men to midwife the birth of the monster.

Four fifteen, and nothing yet that one could see. Maybe it had failed. At least, then, the husbands were safe. God only knew what this strange thing could do to its creators. The men down there, standing before the unknown, might never come home.

Four thirty. The gray dawn rising in the east, and still no sign that the labor and the struggle of the past three years meant anything at all. Should one go to bed? It hardly seemed worthwhile to stand here, scanning the sky, cold and afraid.

Five o'clock. Five fifteen. Then it came. The blinding light like no other light one had ever seen. The trees, illuminated, leaping out at one. The mountains flashing into life. Later, the long, slow rumble. Oh, something has happened, all right, for good or for ill. Something wonderful. Something terrible. The women waiting there in the cold are a part of it. The atomic bomb has been born.

This is the story of the women who watched that first test of the atomic bomb from their home in Los Alamos, New Mexico, more than one hundred and fifty miles north of the desert proving ground. At no other time and at no other place than Los Alamos has such a community mushroomed in secrecy, so apart from the world, yet with a purpose so significant that the world itself would be irrevocably changed by the product of its labor.

This is the story of three years of working and marrying and dying, of giving birth, of getting drunk, of laughing and crying, which culminated in that successful test at the Alamogordo bombing range. It is the story of Los Alamos. In a sense, it is history.

J.S.W.

RUTH MARSHAK

During the greater part of her stay at Los Alamos, Ruth Marshak taught third grade in the Los Alamos School. She also worked in the Housing Office. Her husband, Robert Marshak, was Deputy Head of a theoretical physics group. Before going west to work on the Los Alamos Project, Dr. and Mrs. Marshak were in Montreal where British research along the same lines was being conducted. After Los Alamos, Dr. Robert Marshak became an Associate Professor of Physics at the University of Rochester.

The Marshaks stayed at the University of Rochester for 25 years. During those years, Ruth taught in primary school and reared two children. In 1970 the Marshaks moved to New York City, where Robert became President of City College. Ruth earned a Master of Arts degree in remedial reading, did volunteer work at a child development center in Harlem, and carried out the duties of a college president's wife. In 1979 the Marshaks moved to Blacksburg, Virginia. While Ruth took up gardening, knitting, and reading, Robert was a Distinguished University Professor and taught at Virginia Tech and State University. In September 1987 the Marshaks retired. They continue to live in Blacksburg. Their two children are married and pursuing their own careers. Ann is an Associate Professor in immunology at Boston University Medical School. Steve is an Assistant Professor in Geology at the University of Illinois. The Marshaks have three grandchildren.

1
SECRET CITY

Ruth Marshak

A physicist's wife in peacetime and a physicist's wife in wartime are, I have discovered, two very different things. In the years before our country was at war, this wife's interests were identical with those of any other academic lady. She went to faculty teas, fretted over her budget, and schemed for her husband's advancement. Although a physicist was inclined to work rather longer hours than his colleagues in other departments of the university, his wife's life was no different from that of the wife of a history professor. It was a good life, too.

Even before the Pearl Harbor attack, however, the physicist's routine had changed. Defense projects were started in college laboratories; armed guards began to pace the thresholds of physics buildings. One's husband grew more secretive about his work, and one knew that his job must be important, for he was immune from the draft. The physicist's wife realized that her husband, in wartime, was more than just a college professor—his was a key profession in the defense of his country.

Some physicists remained at home to teach the few students who were left in the universities. Others worked on subcontracts for the Army or the Navy in their own laboratories. But many were forced to leave home in order to do their part in developing and perfecting the weapons of war. They went to a giant installation at the Massachusetts Institute of Technology to work on radar. They went to Washington as Naval Ordnance men. They went to the Aberdeen Proving Grounds. Then, sometimes, the wives who accompanied them found that they were moving to a destination without a name.

1

I was one of the women thus bound for an unknown and secret place. "I can tell you nothing about it," my husband said. "We're going away, that's all." This made me feel a little like the heroine of a melodrama. It is never easy to say goodbye to beloved and familiar patterns of living. It is particularly difficult when you do not know what substitute for them will be offered you. Where was I going and why was I going there? I plied my husband with questions which he steadfastly refused to answer.

"Be very careful what you say," he warned me over and over again. As if I, confused and distraught, knew anything which might be of aid and comfort to the enemy! German agents could probably tell me a thing or two, I reflected bitterly. I went about my packing in a daze. Many questions quivered on my lips, but I would have to wait two years to find out most of their answers. "What's it all about?" I cried to my husband. "At least tell me why we are going away?"—That was in 1943, and only when an atomic bomb ripped Hiroshima in the fall of 1945 did I really understand.

When I left home, I had never even heard the name, "Los Alamos." I gradually became aware, however, that we were going to the Southwest. My husband had received a letter of instructions which said, in part, "Go to 109 East Palace Street, Santa Fe, New Mexico. There you will find out how to complete your trip." What should I expect? Rattlesnakes? Outdoor privies? My concern as a housewife over the mechanics of living seemed rather petty in the face of the secrecy surrounding our destination. I felt akin to the pioneer women accompanying their husbands across the uncharted plains westward, alert to danger, resigned to the fact that they journeyed, for weal or for woe, into the Unknown. The analogy is incomplete, for I rode, not in a covered wagon, but in a red coupe, comfortably, over silver highways. The hazards of the road were not Indians but the broken glass that menaced our thin, irreplaceable tires.

Just before reaching New Mexico, we stopped at a gasoline station in Colorado. The attendant looked over the loaded car, examined our license plates, and asked us where we were heading. We replied that we were bound for New Mexico. The man studied my husband and said, "Oh, you folks must be going to that secret project!" He needed no encouragement to launch into a detailed and accurate description of our new home. Thus for my husband's caution! We proceeded on our way, feeling considerably less important.

We arrived in Santa Fe dusty, tired, and hungry. The Plaza, the antiquity of the architecture, the Indians hawking their wares—all were just as we had imagined they might be. Too much cannot be said for the poetic gesture which placed that fantastic settlement, Los Alamos, in that fantastic state, New Mexico. Santa Fe is the second oldest town in the United States, and its various racial and cultural strata have never quite jelled. There are Indian pueblos nearby with civilizations that were old in Coronado's time and have changed but little since. The predominant racial stock in Santa Fe and the country around it is Spanish-American. These people are descendants of the conquistadores, have some Indian blood certainly, but still are completely different from the Indians in both appearance and customs. They till the soil much as their ancestors did centuries ago. I was to find both kinds of "natives" working at Los Alamos, and they gave a remarkable flair to the place. There they were, the oldest peoples of America, conservative, unchanged, barely touched by our industrial civilization, working on a project with an object so radical that it would be hailed as initiating a new age. The Indians and Spanish-Americans of New Mexico were the most unlikely of all peoples to be ushers to the atomic epoch.

The day after we arrived in Santa Fe, we went to 109 East Palace for our passes. We received our instructions from Mrs. McKibbin, who was in charge of the office. I learned nothing new, really. I had already realized that when my husband joined the Manhattan Project it would be as if we shut a great door behind us. The world I had known of friends and family would no longer be real to me. Why, my parents were not even allowed to come to Santa Fe on a pleasure trip! The only bridge between us would be the shadowy one of censored letters. By a rapid transmutation, my husband and I had become different people. He could not even admit that he was a physicist; his profession was "engineer." Now we were part of the top secret of the war, that great secret which lay behind our innocent rural address: P.O. Box 1663, Santa Fe, New Mexico.

P.O. Box 1663 went by many names. Those who lived there were inclined to call it Los Alamos or the mesa. People in Santa Fe referred to it as the Hill. In Manhattan District jargon it was known as Site Y, and although another designation, Zia Project, never really caught on, everyone said, familiarly, "Here on *the* Project." A mournful GI once wailed, "Lost—almost," and the populace laughed, but few called it that. People coming to the Project often spoke of it as Shangri-La.

The first thing I learned about my new home was that it was not, as I had supposed, in the desert, but rather was on the top of a mesa thirty-five miles from Santa Fe. The most direct road to it was a treacherous washboard running through the Indian pueblo of San Ildefonso, over the muddy Rio Grande, and then up a series of narrow switchbacks. As we neared the top of the mesa, the view was breathtaking. Behind us lay the Sangre de Cristo Mountains, at sunset bathed in changing waves of color—scarlets and lavenders. Below was the desert with its flatness broken by majestic palisades that seemed like the ruined cathedrals and palaces of some old, great, vanished race. Ahead was Los Alamos, and beyond the flat plateau on which it sat was its backdrop, the Jemez Mountain Range. Whenever things went wrong at Los Alamos, and there was never a day when they didn't, we had this one consolation—we had a view.

A mile or two before reaching the settlement itself, we had to show our temporary passes to the MP on duty. He jotted our pass and car license numbers on the record for the day. Passes were to be a solemn business in our lives. A lost pass meant hours of delay in the guard's hutment, an elemental little structure, its stark walls decorated with starkly naked pinup girls. The expiration date of a pass was apt to

The most direct road . . . was a treacherous washboard running through the Indian pueblo of San Ildefonso, over the muddy Rio Grande, and then up by a series of narrow switchbacks. (Los Alamos Historical Museum)

My first impression was discouraging. The rickety houses looked like the tenements of a metropolitan slum area; washing hung everywhere, and the garbage cans were over-flowing. (Los Alamos National Laboratory)

creep up, finding one unaware on just the day one had planned an outing. Many a tearful woman or belligerent gent found themselves stopped at the guardhouse, while the rest of the party sailed gaily by. The fence penning Los Alamos was erected and guarded to keep out the treasonable, the malicious, and the curious. This fence had a real effect on the psychology of the people behind it. It was a tangible barrier, a symbol of our isolated lives. Within it lay the most secret part of the atomic bomb project. Los Alamos was a world unto itself, an island in the sky.

So we arrived at the place we would call home. My first impression was discouraging. The rickety houses looked like the tenements of a metropolitan slum area; washing hung everywhere, and the garbage cans were overflowing. Dust rose in great clouds around our car. Later, we learned that the homes were not as hideous as they had seemed at first. Often, they had large yards and attractive interiors. Always, the mountains were behind them, and there was no time of year when the mountains were not beautiful.

The land on which these unsightly temporary shelters had been erected had once constituted the site of the Los Alamos Ranch School for Boys, a rather exclusive and expensive institution. The fine rustic buildings of the school still stood. Fuller Lodge, the boys' dining hall, had become a restaurant for the new tenants, the "engineers." The classrooms had been converted into a Post Exchange. The rest of the original buildings were used as residences, facetiously tagged "Bathtub Row" because they were the only private homes on the mesa possessing these conveniences. Even though houses on Bathtub Row were rat-ridden and in many particulars less convenient than the government-built housing, there was social prestige in living there. More than one acrimonious battle was fought to determine who might move to the Row.

The Housing Office was in one of the Ranch School buildings, and it was the Housing Office which we new, confused arrivals sought on our first morning. Locating any place on the mesa was difficult; the sprawling town had grown rapidly and haphazardly, without order or plan. Roughly in the center of town was Ashley Pond, a shallow little pool, with the laboratories on the one side and the hospital on the other. To the west stretched a section of four- and eight-family dwellings, identical in appearance, hunter green in hue. This section terminated in tight rows of barracks, housing for the enlisted military personnel, which overlooked the horse pasture. East of the pond was the oldest housing, consisting of green duplexes for childless couples, four-family houses for larger families, and Bathtub Row. Adjacent to these relatively luxurious dwellings was the most meager housing on the Hill, a new section known as Morganville. When we finally found the Housing Office, it was to discover with sinking hearts that we were slated to live in one of white frame Morgan buildings. From the beginning, the Housing Office played an important part in everyone's life. Although its primary function was to allocate houses to newcomers and to relocate those whose family was increasing, its services also included providing the Indian maids, running an express agency, and maintaining the houses.

The office had been notified of our arrival. GI furniture had been installed in our new home. We had been given the bare essentials: couch, chairs, table, cots, and bedding. Although GI furniture was occasionally quite attractive, it was never comfortable. The Army cots were particularly hard. It was unfortunate, in a way, that so many people relied on the Army for their furniture. One entered identical houses to gaze with boredom upon practically identical interiors.

The passes we had received in Santa Fe were good for only twenty-four hours. Hence, one of the first things we had to do was to visit

AA Form No. 1

WAR DEPARTMENT
UNITED STATES ENGINEER OFFICE
P. O. BOX 1539
SANTA FE, NEW MEXICO

July 17, .1943

TO R. F. Bacher

Dear Sir:

You have been assigned Housekeeping Quarters in Building
Number **T-120 C**   for which a monthly rental charge of
$ **67 -**   will be made, effective **July 14, 1943**
194 **3** , payable in the Administration Building, Finance
Section, at the end of each month, in cash, or check made
payable to the Treasurer of the United States.

Fixed charges for utilities furnished this set of quarters
will be $ **12.85**   per month.

Fuel Oil, if used in cooking ranges, will be charged for as
consumed at $ **0.09**   per gallon. (See Note below)
NOTE - Utility and fuel oil charges will be payable at the end
of each month in the same manner as indicated above for the
rental charge. The utility and fuel oil charges are subject to
change, if the cost records indicate the necessity therefor.

For the Commanding Officer:

N. E. Davis
Capt., Corps of Engineers,
Assistant.

A housing assignment. (Original provided by Jean Bacher)

the Pass Office. The procedure here struck me as similar to that which a criminal undergoes when he visits a police station. We were finger-printed and photographed and informed once more—but not for the last time—of the need for secrecy. We were forbidden to tell anyone the exact location of the Project, its size, or the number of people living in it. We were told not to mention the names of the scientists who worked there. We signed the Espionage Act. Then we were given new temporary passes and told to report back in two weeks for our permanent ones.

Our tiny half of the duplex in Morganville was scarcely adequate for even a family of two. We had a bedroom, a small living room, a minute kitchen, and a bathroom with a shower but no tub. There was little closet space, no kitchen door, and no lock on the bathroom door. Morganville houses were set in neat parallel rows. There were no trees in our section of the mesa, and the unpaved roads were muddy during wet seasons and dusty during dry ones. Eventually we moved to one of the older green duplexes; compared to our Morganville residence, it was luxurious.

Los Alamos is about 7200 feet above sea level. Many people found the altitude a bit uncomfortable at first. Typical manifestations were a shortness of breath and insomnia. I happened to feel fine, but the altitude affected my cooking and baking. It took much longer for water

Morganville houses were set in neat parallel rows. There were no trees in our section of the mesa, and the unpaved roads were muddy during wet seasons and dusty during dry ones. (Los Alamos Historical Museum)

to boil, so my first few meals were on the tardy side. Cakes rose beautifully in the oven, but fell magically the moment they were removed. I'd never enjoyed baking anyhow, so I now had an excuse not to bake at all. There were, however, no commercial bakeries on the Hill.

After one grew acclimated to the altitude, one began really to enjoy the Los Alamos climate. Los Alamos was a secret place, and the job of its large Security Division was to avoid publicity, not to court it. Had it had a Chamber of Commerce or a bigger booster club, however, wonderful advertisements might have been written about its weather. The sun shone almost every day. Although summer days might be warm, they were never unendurable, for the air was dry. Winters were without penetrating cold. The citizens of our community seemed to draw vigor from the air. They not only worked inhuman hours to perfect the bomb; they also had energy to dissipate on skiing and horseback riding, mountain climbing and folk dancing, and gay parties which lasted until dawn.

The social life of the Hill was surely one of its redeeming features. I found much friendliness and informality, but I discovered also that Los Alamos was not a casteless society. Lines were drawn principally, not on wealth, family, or even age, but on the position one's husband held in the Laboratory.

There was quite a social cleavage between the military and the scientific personnel. The scientists' position as civilians on an Army Post was an anomalous one. They differed with the Army administration on a number of matters, the crux of all disputes being who was boss and should determine policy, the Army or the scientists. We certainly could not have maintained the settlement without Army priorities. The scientists depended on the Army for laboratory equipment, for food, for construction, for maintenance, for the thousand things necessary in building and sustaining a new community. But the very reason for Los Alamos' existence was its laboratory, and a laboratory cannot function properly except under scientific control. As a result of these conflicting interests, authority was divided. The commanding officer of the Post was a Colonel of the U.S. Engineers; he not only was responsible for the other Army engineers, but also was CO for the Wacs, the Special Engineer Detachment (Army technicians who worked in the Laboratory), and a large force of Military Police stationed on the mesa. Under his aegis were the civilians concerned with the town, including clerks in the stores and PXs, bookkeepers, furnace men, road builders, construction gangs, and firemen.

Los Alamos was the only project connected with the atomic bomb which was actually an Army Post, but all the projects operated under the War Department. It now seems to be common knowledge that few scientists cared for the military man who administered the Project, Major General Leslie Groves. It was convenient, of course, to blame someone for our ills. Groves was an authority on Congressional investigations, and some of us thought that this was one reason he had been chosen for this job. Had the atomic bomb not materialized, there was always the possibility of Congress investigating the reason why millions and millions of dollars had been spent on a boondoggle.

So we lived in anticipation of a Congressional investigation, and we felt that Groves was parsimonious with us civilians. We could not have street lights, which seemed to us scarcely an extravagance where there was so much reckless traffic. People said that one reason for the constant construction and expansion at Los Alamos was that Groves did not have to approve expenditures under a certain sum. Thus a small, inexpensive annex to a building could be erected during one month, and an annex to that annex built the next.

The Laboratory, or rather the group of laboratories, known as the Technical Area, Tech Area, or more laconically as Tech, was directed by J. Robert Oppenheimer, a young and brilliant theoretical physicist from the University of California. Special passes and badges were required for admission into this most secret place, the community's very reason for being. The fence that surrounded it was heavily guarded. Through its gates went the experimental and theoretical physicists, the chemists, the metallurgists, the ordnance experts, the engineers, and the administrators who worked there. Each department under Dr. Oppenheimer was a hierarchy with a division leader in charge. Group leaders in each division tackled special problems and supervised the work of the younger scientists and technicians.

The Tech Area was a great pit which swallowed our scientist husbands out of sight, almost out of our lives. The men were drawn to their work not only by curiosity and zeal, but also by an inspiring patriotism. They worked as they had never worked before. They worked at night and often came home at three or four in the morning. Sometimes, they set up Army cots in the laboratories and did not come home at all. Other times, they did not sleep at all. Few women understood

The Tech Area was a great pit which swallowed our scientist husbands out of sight, almost out of our lives. . . . They worked as they had never worked before. . . . The loneliness and heartache of some scientists' wives during the years before the atomic bomb was born were very real. (Los Alamos National Laboratory)

what the men were seeking there or comprehended the magnitude of the search. The loneliness and heartache of some scientists' wives during the years before the atomic bomb was born were very real.

There was some compensation in the fact that the mesa was Celebrity Land. To many scientists, Los Alamos stood for the same sort of thing that Hollywood represents to an aspiring starlet. Most of the great men of physics and chemistry were there at one time or another. Niels Bohr, A. H. Compton, I. I. Rabi, Harold Urey, E. O. Lawrence, and James B. Conant arrived, often for protracted visits. Enrico Fermi, Italian Nobel Prize winner, lived at Los Alamos. So did Sir James Chadwick, an English Nobel Prize man.

Los Alamos was an interesting experience, partly because of the personalities involved. It was a small town where private matters were of public concern, yet it was an unusual small town because so many of its citizens were brilliant men and women—many with the peculiarities attendant upon brilliance.

The community was designed to be self-sustaining, and that it really was so to any degree was something of a triumph. There were large gaps, however, and a shopping expedition to Santa Fe every month or so was mandatory for most families. The one general store on the mesa opened business with remnants from the Los Alamos Ranch School Trading Post. To a populace hungry for goods, it offered small boys' T-shirts, boys' moccasins, boys' underwear, and little else. Although the stock was finally expanded to include ornate bric-a-brac, it was never adequate. Montgomery Ward catalogues—but not those of Sears Roebuck—were available in the store. The civilians murmured among themselves that this discrimination existed because the captain in charge of the Trading Post had been a Montgomery Ward employee before the war.

We had one Commissary on the mesa, and there were sharp differences of opinion as to how cheap or how good it was. Many of the national shortages hit us until we were groggy. We had, as well, a flurry of local shortages unique, as far as I know, to Los Alamos. Fruits and vegetables, doubtless weary and ailing to begin with, made the long trek up from Santa Fe and expired on the Commissary shelves. Fresh eggs were never available, but after the housewives howled for months, the Post veterinarian candled each egg before it was sold. Canned goods often went unlabeled, and when brands could be identified, they were usually unfamiliar. Meat, on the other hand, was good and remarkably inexpensive. The clerks were sometimes soldiers, sometimes civilians, and I am under the impression that the purchasing was also done in a somewhat irregular manner—sometimes through the Quartermaster Corps of the Army, sometimes through civilian channels.

There were two Post Exchanges at Los Alamos, both selling bad meals and warm Coca-Colas to the accompaniment of juke box music. Despite the fact that they sold only 3.2 beer, they were our local Sodoms and Gomorrahs. Drives to prevent juvenile delinquency always aimed at the exclusion of young people from the PXs at night. I don't think anything ever happened at these places which might start a youngster on a life of crime. The PXs did seem disreputable at night, though; they were crowded, smoky, and noisy.

Besides the PXs, one could eat at Fuller Lodge, which would serve splendid food for a few months and then slump back to its usual standard of mediocre cooking. There also were two civilian mess halls

Canned goods often went unlabeled, and when brands could be identified, they were usually unfamiliar. (Los Alamos Historical Museum)

One could eat at Fuller Lodge, which would serve splendid food for a few months and then slump back to its usual standard of mediocre cooking. (Los Alamos Historical Museum)

about which I can, after a great deal of thought, find only one kind thing to say: they were cheap. The cafeteria was a much later and much better development. For once, something was large enough for our needs and did not require an annex the month after it had been built. It was a pleasant place in which to eat. Once a week was "steak night," and with those inch-thick filet mignons costing one dollar, cuisine at Los Alamos reached its all-time peak.

Before the town was really a going concern, the Army instituted a beauty parlor, doubtless for morale reasons. The barber shop, a later development, was criticized for its inadequate facilities. It is hard for a man to wait an hour to have his hair cut at any time; it is almost impossible when he is working under the kind of pressure which drove most of the scientists at Los Alamos. In exasperation, one young group leader in the Tech Area stuck into his order blank along with requests for switches, Geiger counters, and other implements of his trade, the request for a barber chair. Because there actually was an old barber chair in the warehouse, the Procurement Department, with tongue in cheek, sent it down to him. The young man set it near the cyclotron, and the boys on the atom-smashing crews began testing their barbering talents on one another. Friends in Tech eyed this new experiment with interest and donated such items as a *Police Gazette*, talc, and cologne. They even flocked to the cyclotron to have their hair cut. After General Groves, on one of his periodic tours, had eyed this "barber shoppe" of the Tech Area, the Post barber shop acquired several more chairs and enlarged its staff.

Other services were instituted gradually. We acquired a garage and a dry-cleaning establishment. I cannot sing the praises of these monopolies. Certainly, having them was better than going without, but they were not models of their type.

Laundry could be sent to Santa Fe to some of the most absentminded commercial laundries in the U.S.A., or it could be done on the site in a communal self-service laundry. There were five of these, situated in various sections of the mesa. Here one could rent a washing machine, a hand iron, or a mangle by the hour. Diapers could be sent to a diaper service operated by the desperate mothers themselves with a great deal of attendant misery.

There were two theaters at Los Alamos where one could sit on hard seats and see a movie for fifteen cents. They served more than double duty. They were gymnasiums, dance halls, and, respectively, Catholic

There were two civilian mess halls . . . they were cheap. The cafeteria was a much later and much better development. (Los Alamos Historical Museum)

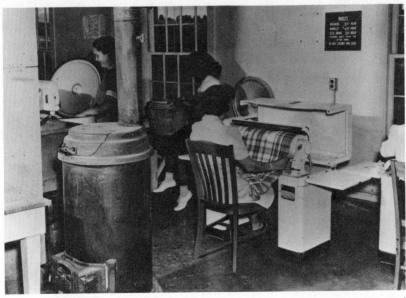

Laundry could be sent to Santa Fe . . . or it could be done on the site in a communal self-service laundry. (Los Alamos Historical Museum)

and Protestant churches. Chaplain Matthew Imrie came to the Project after we had had quite a period without religious guidance. Scientists are, by and large, indifferent churchgoers, but the chaplain performed some weddings and a few christenings for us. Through his efforts the young people of the community obtained a youth center, and the Army began subsidizing a cooperative lending library, which had languished under poverty. The library, as well as the amateur orchestras, amateur choral groups, and amateur theatricals of Los Alamos, was a result of the spontaneous efforts of private citizens to make of this barren Army Post some sort of real home. In the same way, from the early days of the Project, we enjoyed a local radio station manned by volunteers. It specialized in classical music and newscasts, had no commercials, and in general catered to the taste of its rather special public. Records were donated or lent to the station, which seemed to support itself on no budget at all.

We complained. We complained bitterly. There was much about which to complain. But in the bitter barrage we civilians often threw at the administration, there were few criticisms of the hospital. The doctors were competent and popular. Many drugs were free. Medical and dental care were gratis. When one stayed in the hospital, there was a charge, all right—a dollar a day for food! Perhaps it was to take advantage of this opportunity that so many babies were born at Los Alamos, or perhaps it was because the population was so youthful. The General was reputed to have complained to Dr. Oppenheimer about the number of children being born on the Hill. Couldn't something be done about it, the General wanted to know. A jingle celebrating this remark went in part:

> The General's in a stew
> He trusted you and you
> He thought you'd be scientific
> Instead you're just prolific
> And what is he to do?

For local government, we had an elected body called the Town Council. Since the Town Council could only make recommendations to the military administration, it was scarcely a potent force. However, it was the necessary outlet for steam when things became too impossible. It did a great deal of good, too. Particularly in the beginning, elections were attended by considerable excitement. Town Council was only another instance of individual participation and interest in group affairs.

From the very beginning of the Project, Los Alamos had a fire department. At first its personnel was civilian; later, in typical Los Alamos fashion, the fire department was composed of soldiers under a civilian fire chief. Situated as we were in arid country, surrounded by pine forests, living in firetrap buildings, fire was always a hazard. Actually, we had only one serious fire in three years on the site. The furnaces of the houses frequently exploded, however, and some minor fires did occur. Our houses were numbered in a completely random way, and all those of one building development looked so similar that a drunk could have real trouble locating his own mansion. In case of fire, therefore, the fire department was often confused, and firemen would dash up and down streets all over the mesa, taking an unconscionable length of time to locate the burning building.

I was particularly interested in the school because I taught there. The building was painted the same bilious green as the surrounding

The [school] building was painted the same bilious green as the surrounding residences, but it offered an unexcelled view of the Jemez Mountains. (Los Alamos National Laboratory)

residences, but it offered an unexcelled view of the Jemez Mountains beyond its great plate windows. Rock had been blasted to lay its foundation, and it had been expensive to build. The teaching staff for the large elementary section and the small high school section was recruited from women already on the Hill whenever possible. It was supervised, in an absentminded way, by a school board composed of scientific personnel and Army officers who met as seldom as they could. They felt that they had more important things on their minds than the school, as they doubtless had. Meanwhile, during its first three years of existence, the school had four superintendents and once, for a long, disorganized term, had no superintendent at all. Since the various supervisors all had different theories of education, a teacher at Los Alamos had to be flexible. During the spring semester she might find herself a conservative instructor of the fundamentals, while in the fall

The teaching staff for the large elementary section and the small high school section was recruited from women already on the Hill whenever possible. . . . Since the various supervisors all had different theories of education, a teacher at Los Alamos had to be flexible. During the spring semester she might find herself a conservative instructor of the fundamentals, while in the fall she might teach under the most avant-garde methods of progressive education. (Los Alamos National Laboratory)

she might teach under the most avant-garde methods of progressive education.

We teachers worked under difficulties. When an experimental blast in a nearby canyon would rock the school to its expensive foundation, there would be a frightened silence in the classroom, and then we would begin again on Henry Wadsworth Longfellow. The school furnace was subject to the same idiosyncrasies as our furnaces at home. Sometimes there was no heat, and the youngsters sat in class bundled up in overcoats and galoshes. More often, the furnace blasted, the furnace roared, and I taught in a sticky atmosphere of 90 degrees Fahrenheit. It struck me as significant, if not symbolic, that in our school the electric clocks occasionally ran backwards.

The school had been set up by a professor of education from the University of Minnesota. He had shaped a rigidly academic curriculum for the high school under the impression that a group of brilliant children of brilliant scientists would be taught there. Since the average age of the scientists at Los Alamos during the pre-Hiroshima years was all of twenty-seven, it is not surprising that most of the high school kids came from nonprofessional homes. Some secondary students did not feel at ease under the college preparatory curriculum, but with only three full-time teachers not much else could be offered to them. Even so, I have since heard about many students who have returned to more normal schools in more ordinary communities. They appear to be doing very well, indeed. If anything, their scholarship has been enriched by their years in our unconventional little green schoolhouse.

In a broader sense, for most of us elders, the Los Alamos experience was one of the most educational of our lives. Sequestered, regimented, we had to make the most of the little we had. Perhaps it was a good thing, three years ago when I left home and started westward, that I knew so little of what awaited me. There was much amiss in the ugly town where the bomb was born. Yet I have only to think of the neighborliness and warmth and esprit de corps of Los Alamos to be heartily glad for the chance that took me there. Nor is it surprising that most people enjoyed their years on the mesa. Los Alamos was our town, our own creation. To no other community will we ever give so much of ourselves.

—at 109 East Palace.

DOROTHY McKIBBIN

Dorothy McKibbin was a Santa Fe resident. She lived in an adobe house opposite the Laboratory of Anthropology, and her past life had little to do with scientists and their worries. She worked for the Project from the first days of the Santa Fe office and was of tremendous value because of her thorough knowledge of the surrounding country.

After twenty years with the Laboratory, Dorothy retired in 1963. Scientists she had met in her office at 109 East Palace continued to be among her closest friends, and more than twenty Los Alamos couples were married in her home on Old Santa Fe Trail, a tradition begun when wartime restrictions disrupted previous wedding conventions. In 1980 Dorothy received an honorary degree from the College of Santa Fe. That occasion was especially significant because others similarly honored included María Martinez, the potter of San Ildefonso, and Harold Agnew, a former Director of the Laboratory at Los Alamos—two old friends from the two worlds she loved. Dorothy died in Santa Fe in 1985.

2

109 EAST PALACE

Dorothy McKibbin

109 East Palace was the Los Alamos Santa Fe office which served as a reception desk, information center, and travel bureau. Scientists arrived there breathless, sleepless, and haggard, tired from riding on trains that were slow and trains that were crowded, tired from missing connections and having nothing to eat, or tired from waiting out the dawn hours in a railroad station. Often the traveler arrived days after he had been expected and settled down with a sigh into a chair at 109 East Palace as if he could never move again. One could almost see his fatigue dropping off and piling up against the old adobe walls.

Most of the new arrivals were tense with expectancy and curiosity. They had left physics, chemistry, and metallurgical laboratories, had sold their homes or rented them, had deceived their friends, and then had launched forth into an unpredictable world. They walked into the thick-walled quietness of the old Spanish dwelling at 109 East Palace expecting anything and everything, the best and the worst.

The scientists often arrived in a frantic hurry. One dashed in hatless and breathless after a hectic rush from Johns Hopkins University and panted in dismay, "What, no ride up for an hour and a half? Why, I cut short a seminar in order to get here now!"

"Up" meant, to the Project members, those thirty-five miles to the site at Los Alamos. The site was universally called "the Hill" in Santa Fe. Sometimes we called it upstairs, but the Hill really stuck. The elevation of the Project was practically the same as that of Santa Fe, but the road between them dropped down into Tesuque, past Cuyamungue, and into the Nambe and Rio Grande valleys before it climbed

"Up" meant, to the Project members, those thirty-five miles to the site at Los Alamos. . . .
The elevation of the Project was practically the same as that of Santa Fe, but the road
between them dropped down into Tesuque, past Cuyamungue, and into the Nambe
and Rio Grande valleys before it climbed the last steep ten miles to regain the lost altitude.
(Los Alamos Historical Museum)

the last steep ten miles to regain the lost altitude. The site rested on
the flat mesas extending eastward from the Jemez Range.

Before going up, the atomic scientist was welcomed within the old
walls of 109 East Palace, the oldest building east of the Governor's
Palace in that part of Santa Fe. True, the calcimine on the walls was
new, so new that it came off onto his coat if he leaned against it. The
furniture was government issue. But the scientist hesitated among
those old walls only long enough to get a pass to take him past the
ancient cliff dwelling ruins and on to the plateau and its incredible
laboratories.

A yellow map was inscribed for the new arrival, with red pencil
marking every mile and every turn of his route up. He proceeded in
his own car, in a staff car, or in one of the gargantuan Army buses
parked outside, waiting to hurl their exhaust blasts in a rolling staccato
at the shaky old *portal*.

The road winds near the pueblos of Santa Clara and San Ildefonso
and after it leaves the valley of the Rio Grande it begins to climb. Large

lava beds are visible, and black escarpments. Then, salmon-colored cliffs, clean and high, tower to the sky. The trees are taller, and the earth smells of pine needles. Leaving the black lava on one side, the road runs under tent-rock formations and cuts through a white pumice bed. The Jemez Range is of volcanic formation, so the tuff is soft and easy to cut. Many ruins of ancient cliff dwellings lie near the road, Tsankawi, Tsirege, Frijoles, Puye, and many more as yet unnamed. The ruins of Otowi appear last as the road mounts to the top and runs past the guardhouse and on up to the scientific laboratories. The town is humming with rush and hurry, and military cars swarm all over its winding roads. Buildings have been erected overnight, and they look it.

When the Tech Area administrative staff arrived in March 1943, they stayed in Santa Fe until the buildings on the Hill were finished. They took over five offices at 109 East Palace and functioned there full blast until the end of April. Army guards crept around these offices and stood in the shadow of the *portales* day and night. The Director's office and the offices of the Business Manager, Procurement and Personnel were hives of activity. Telephones rang constantly, and since few lines were connected interoffice, secretaries chased from office to office to drag the person being called to the waiting telephone.

Since the housing, as well as the offices, on the Hill had not been completed, the Project rented four ranches within twenty miles of Santa Fe, and as the eager scientists arrived, they were assigned with their families to the ranches. The laboratories at the site were in a sketchy state, but that did not deter the workers. In the morning, buses (which could be station wagons, sedans, or trucks) left 109 to pick up the men at the ranches and take them to the Hill. Occasionally a driver forgot to stop at a ranch, and the stranded and frustrated scientist would call in a white heat. Because there was no way to get food up there for their lunches, we had box lunches prepared in Santa Fe and taken up for the noon hour. The restaurants must have thought there was a tremendous amount of picnicking going on somewhere.

In June, staff members were moved from the ranches and housed either on the Hill or at Frijoles Lodge. The Lodge, an isolated mountain inn situated in the Bandelier National Monument in the Jemez Range, was taken over by the Project because it was closer than the ranches and the workers could commute to the Hill more easily and less conspicuously. *Los Ritos de los Frijoles* is the site of old cliff dwellings and huge pueblo ruins, and the kivas and ceremonial cave had many an interested visitor that summer. By the end of summer, the apartments and dormitories were completed and all members of the technical staff were housed on the Hill.

Meanwhile, by the end of April all the offices at 109 except mine had been picked up and moved to the Hill. A variety of functions remained in Santa Fe: the buses departed from here and therefore 109 became a center for the shoppers from the Hill; it was and still is an information center, not too accurate, but always willing, for inquiries on how and where to get items ranging from horses to hair ribbons. Babies were parked here. Dogs were tied outside. Our trucks delivered baggage, express, and freight to the Hill, and even special orders of flowers, hot rolls, baby cribs, and pumpernickel.

Of all the incoming personnel, the Wacs and some of the soldiers were at their lowest ebb in this office. They had not been told what was going to happen to them. They had been alerted for overseas duty, and the overseas silence had been flung around the shoulders of their families. They were ectoplasm for about five days without even an APO number. One Wac told me she was not allowed to mention to her closest buddy the fact that she was going overseas and was whisked out of her cot at two A.M. to be sent silently on her way. When the train ran west and stopped at Lamy, she thought it was all a big mistake, since the sand and piñon trees did not look like any ocean she had ever seen. The nightmare continued when she walked into an old mud building which had nothing marine about it and was told that she had thirty-five miles farther to go into "that beat-up land." Many Wacs were tearful in those early days. They were good soldiers, but the shock was too much for them. Quite a few have I ushered gently into Army cars or buses and sent on their way weeping. Soldiers also had no further orders than Santa Fe, and they too were confused and apprehensive.

Tired families with small babies came in and said hopefully that they had sent their furniture to 109, but it didn't look like much of a home. . . .

"Thirty-five miles to go," we told them.

Machinists dashed in and asked, "Where is the dance hall?"

"Thirty-five miles to go."

"Well, I think I will leave my suitcase down here. I may not like it. . . ."

For security reasons, there was never any discussion of the work going on up there, needless to say. I could see that the new arrivals coming into the office for the first time were bursting with curiosity and anticipation. Words were never spoken, but the atmosphere was full of suppressed excitement. It was interesting to see how much the different types of employees knew about where they were going and what it was like when they first arrived. Many came in the greatest ignorance and were correspondingly astonished and confused.

For security reasons, also, the word "physicist" was taboo. If there was no stranger around and I was feeling very wicked, I would glance in all directions, examine the empty air, raise an eyebrow, and whisper tensely, blowing through my teeth like a suppressed wind instrument, "Are you a phhh ht?"

Some of the most famous physicists traveled under assumed names. We never spoke of anyone by the term Doctor or Professor, but always called him Mister. We never mentioned the names of Project people to anyone except Project members.

One day Dr. Enrico Fermi and Dr. Sam Allison were in the office waiting for a car to take them to the Hill. As I made out their passes, I tossed my head and informed them that we had to demote them down here and speak of them and to them as plain Mister. They strolled around the town while waiting. Near the Cathedral, they noticed a statue in the yard.

"Who is that?" asked Allison of Fermi.

"That is Archbishop Lamy," said Fermi.

"Shhhh," whispered Allison, grabbing Fermi's arm and glancing around cautiously. "Mrs. McKibbin would suggest we call him *Mr.* Lamy."

One bright afternoon I had a call from the Hill asking me if I saw anything in the sky that might be a Japanese balloon. The object was situated so many degrees from the sun, etc., and they had been observing it from the site and would like to know how it appeared from Santa Fe. I bustled out and scanned the skies from the Plaza and then drove to the top of old Fort Marcy and looked and looked. Apprehension and fear crept around my mind and heart as I contemplated such a possibility, with full knowledge of the danger to the Project. I could not see the object in question, but I did see little puffs of cloud, very frail and tenuous, which formed and reformed like vapor. Each one I imagined to be a small parachute with a missile attached.

I later discovered that a few Japanese balloons had been dropped in the Southwest, putting the staff on the Hill, from the Director down, in a dither that day. While the Army sent up search planes, the scientists spent the afternoon craning their necks and evolving fantastic theories about the phenomenon. The Personnel Director, an astronomer by profession, was called upon in his dual capacity to settle the argument in order to get the staff back to work. Since even he would not make a flat statement, speculation continued until the next day. Again at noon, the same luminescent object appeared in the sky. Only then did the experts agree that it was nothing more nor less than the planet Venus, rarely seen in broad daylight.

Santa Feans soon became accustomed to the queer ways of the scientists. They claimed they could spot these people from a great distance. Frequently, a clerk in a shop, prompted more by western hospitality than by curiosity, automatically inquired, "Where are you from?" The answer was always a stammered "Box 1663," as the speaker faded into the background. Security allowed them to say no more. Santa Feans knew what Box 1663 meant and felt smug about it. They referred to the place as the submarine base, or the place where submarine windshield wipers were made. They knew that inquiries caused acute embarrassment, and often a perfectly natural question froze on their lips.

We had a little trouble with the city police who complained that our huge buses stopped too long outside our door and blocked traffic. The street was narrow and cars were allowed to park on only one side. Of course, we were on the other side. A bus could be a hazard when a fire truck went screeching through the streets, particularly if a car was parked across the street from the bus. The buses were therefore allowed to stand only a short time in order to avoid these crises. Sometimes, if the buses were too few or too late for the waiting mobs, I would be awakened at home in the middle of the night by a telephone call asking, "Where is the bus?" As if I knew . . . !

As most of the business between 109 and the Hill was transacted by telephone, the shortage of lines caused us great difficulty. A scientist rushing into the office in a great hurry before boarding a train would tear his hair while the operator told us endlessly, "line is busy." In the early days, the record time in getting a call through was an hour and a half, and the delay was particularly rugged when someone was waiting on long distance for us to make the contact for him. Now there are many lines, and we no longer have difficulty in getting our numbers.

All kinds, ages, and conditions of people came to 109 seeking employment on the Hill. The personnel work was fascinating. We did some initial interviewing, and if people seemed qualified, they were given extensive applications to fill out. One officer who had been overseas with several different combat units listed his occupation as "murder." A woman who had worked in one of the mess halls listed her "equipment used" as "blue uniform and hair nets."

To work on the Project, new employees had to be cleared by Security. Waiting for clearance was difficult for many people, and we had to go through their agonies with them. The two weeks required to check on them often consumed their funds and their spirits. They were tossed out of hotels every three days, and the scarcity of housing in this Land of Enchantment made the waiting doubly difficult.

Observing a place grow from one hundred to thousands of families is extremely absorbing. I was on excellent terms with many of the scientists and was more aware of their affairs than were most of the people in Santa Fe. There were weddings, divorces, and always many, many births. There was the constant arriving and departing from 109 East Palace. The first year of the Project's existence was celebrated with due ceremony, and then the second. We have now celebrated our third year. Babies who once slept in the office in their bassinets while their mothers shopped are now rushing around my desk and tearing the Scotch tape out of its holder.

When we were employed we were told to ask no questions, and we didn't—much. We worked with pride. We sensed the excitement and suspense of the Project, for the intensity of the people coming through the office was contagious. Working at 109 was more than just a job. It was an exciting experience. Our office served as the entrance to one of the most significant undertakings of the war or, indeed, of the twentieth century.

KATHLEEN MARK

Originally a Canadian, Kathleen (Kay) Mark was born in Toronto, where she lived for 26 years. In 1935 she married Carson Mark, then a graduate student at the University of Toronto. In 1938 they moved to Winnipeg, where Carson taught in the mathematics department of the University of Manitoba until 1943. Three children, Joan, Tom, and Elizabeth were born in Winnipeg. When they moved to Montreal in 1943 Elizabeth was three weeks old. At the Université de Montreal Carson worked in association with George Placzek, and when George moved to Los Alamos in 1945, Carson followed. The rest of the family joined him a couple of months later, after a delay due to the wartime crowding of trains. This time it was Graham who was just a few weeks old. In Los Alamos they lived for a few months in the now-vanished McKee area, before moving to a more commodious Sundt, now also vanished.

In 1947 they moved to the Western Area in Los Alamos, where they still live. Two more children, Christopher and Mary Ellen, completed the family, and the years were busy with family involvements and Carson's complete immersion in the Laboratory. By the 1960s, with more time available, Kay published several children's stories and finally began several years of commuting to the University of New Mexico in Albuquerque to take classes in geology. Since then she has published articles on various geological topics and, most recently, *Meteorite Craters* (The University of Arizona Press, 1987) on the recognition of meteorite craters.

3
A ROOF OVER OUR HEADS

Kathleen Mark

"No doubt this is among the most fantastic of the works of nature," my husband remarked as we rode up the last steep stretches of the road to Los Alamos. The road clung to one pink wall of the canyon, and as we gazed in fascination the sun bronzed the opposite wall all the way from the rubble near the bottom to the old lava pockets near the top. "And in a few minutes," he went on, "you'll see some of the most fantastic of the works of man."

The road, carved out of sheer rock, seemed itself a fantastic work. It wound upward and then suddenly flattened out as we reached the top of the mesa, and the next fantastic work of man came into view in the shape of a small guardhouse in the middle of the road. Here all traffic, whether coming or going, stopped for police inspection; and here, as I later discovered, was a foretaste of Los Alamos architecture. The guardhouse was small, but evidently adequate. Here was shelter for these arms of the law, shelter from the sun and from the rain (if any). Here was a place to sit, a wall on which to pin up whatever was considered appropriate, a door on each side through which to inspect the passes of travelers. Perhaps there were even some small luxuries in addition—though none were evident from the outside. The guardhouse was painted green.

We drove on and soon there were more signs of habitation. Trucks stood in orderly rows behind wire fences, along with jeeps and tractors. Next, there were sheds, painted green. Then suddenly we were in the midst of a conglomeration of small buildings, Army trucks, wire fences, and people. As we drove rapidly through it my impressions were

29

mainly of green paint and lack of height, for there were no trees and no large buildings at this point. We swung into an even more extraordinary setting, and here I had my first glimpse of Los Alamos housing. Standing on each side of the road, lined up side by side with very little space between them—and painted green—were trailers. Some orderly soul with a penchant for filing had sorted them all out and arranged them in groups of a kind. I found the result unbelievably funny. Six or eight trailers, repeating six or eight times a rounded outline, a window, and a small tin chimney, gave place then to several with, say, a square end, a door, and two steps. The pattern was repeated several times, changing again in detail farther down the line while the height and color remained the same.

We whisked through several rows of trailers and then both pattern and color changed. It was as though some mythical being had passed by, sowing as he went not dragons' teeth but—well—latch keys, let us

Standing on each side of the road, lined up side by side with very little space between them—and painted green—were trailers. Some orderly soul with a penchant for filing had sorted them all out and arranged them in groups of a kind. I found the result unbelievably funny. (Los Alamos National Laboratory)

Six or eight trailers, repeating six or eight times a rounded outline, a window, and a small tin chimney, gave place then to several with, say a square end, a door, and two steps. (Los Alamos Historical Museum)

say. Here was the appropriate crop, in the form of neat rows of individual white dwellings. They were like small apartments which owing to some disturbance in their development had grown separately instead of all together in a compact single building and had never therefore acquired a seasoned outer shell. These small boxlike structures, at first glance boasting no sort of individuality, perplexed me: they had been placed beneath a tangled mass of tin chimneys and radio wires. Obviously, each house must contribute two chimneys and one radio wire, and the mass could not be greater than the net total of all contributions. (Such deductions are easy when one's husband is a mathematician.) At first glance, however, I was not inclined to be exactingly logical, and I saw this superstructure of hardware as something almost completely irrelevant to the boxes below it.

"The one at the end," my husband said to the driver. "The one next to the laundry."

Our house looked like all the others, but it was uniquely placed: if I could find my way to the laundry, I'd always be able to get home! We disembarked, and the children rushed in. For a moment I expected to see the poor little house bulge under the impact like a house in a Disney cartoon. It remained rigid, however, even after we were all inside. In spite of its fragile appearance, it contrived to house us all for some months without signs of undue strain.

Our house, I soon learned, was a McKee house, so named after the contractor who built it. Besides an allotment of GI furniture, it contained an oil furnace, an auxiliary oil heater (neither of them objects of beauty), and an oil-burning water heater. I had to swallow my prejudice against oil burners in general—a prejudice that was perhaps ill-founded for no oil burners blew up while we were there or at any other time, as far as I know. True, they were not proof against all contingencies. The brief, violent rain storms which suddenly burst from small innocent-looking clouds in an otherwise serenely blue sky often soaked the tin chimneys and put out the small flame in the water heater. Soot was another thing to be reckoned with. Our furnace, being of a contrary disposition, chose a week when my husband was away and the children had the flu to have a soot attack. I had to peer into its mysterious and filthy interior to convince myself that it really was completely indisposed. Then, as the weather was chilly, I had to light the auxiliary heater. As I am now prepared to admit, this is a very simple matter, but at the time it required set teeth. The auxiliary gave little heat, but it roared and belched all night like a bilious dragon. It was with great relief that I extinguished it in the morning. Eventually, men experienced in such matters came with vacuum cleaners to desoot the furnace, and things returned to normal.

Another feature of the McKee houses was cracks. There were cracks under the window frames, cracks around the door—in fact we never knew how many places had cracks until a dust storm occurred. During a storm, dust and sand came in through the cracks in puffs, in gusts, in clouds, in streams. On the furniture and on the floor, everywhere, was a continuous heavy layer of dust, and here and there were piles like miniature sand dunes. On these occasions one swore softly or loudly, as the case might be, at the cracks, and when the wind dropped one went to work to put the dust outside again, where it stayed until the next time. Having what my friends must find an exasperatingly Pollyanna-ish streak in my makeup, I always derived undue satisfaction from the thought that at least each time it was different dust.

The process of settling into our new groove went on, and I spent part of each day exploring the site. Exploration in company with a baby carriage, a wagon, and three small children was necessarily slow. But it was fun, and soon a pattern began to emerge from the welter of buildings. McKeeville, I discovered, was the most recently built section. Next newest was Morganville, also named after its contractor. The Morgan houses were also painted white, but they were two-family units, with common heating and hot water systems. This, of course, necessitated furnace men, and in this they differed most profoundly from McKee houses. McKeeville at night was merely McKeeville with all its lights out, whereas Morganville at night was something entirely different from Morganville by day. By day the Morganville furnace rooms were partly obscured by coal bins and were not very noticeable; at night they were lit up while the rest of the house slumbered in darkness. In each house, the furnace room glowed gently through the surrounding gloom, and one could distinguish the outline of boiler and pipes and, not infrequently, of congenial furnace men. At night, furnace men really came into their own; at night Morganville was theirs. In the daytime, they were sorrier creatures whose lot it was to listen to countless complaints about overheated water, hot water in cold water taps, hot water even in toilets, thermostats being improperly controlled, fire extinguishers having been locked up in the furnace rooms, and so on. Listen they did, to all this and more, absent-mindedly and humbly sympathetic. But with nightfall these assumed burdens of the community rolled from their shoulders, and the furnace rooms of Morganville became pleasant, cheerful places where furnace men chatted together and played games with something that rattled.

Morganville and McKeeville, being the newest and most obviously mass-produced sections, were perhaps the least interesting. It had been expected originally that the Project might involve as many as five hundred people, and housing had been planned accordingly. Morganville and McKeeville had been hasty though very necessary afterthoughts, for by V-J Day the population was nearer to five thousand.

Scattered over the whole site were dormitories. Most of them were grimly angular buildings, painted green or white, and they ranged from long Pacific huts containing two rows of cots to fairly comfortable two-story affairs. They housed single people, married people who had left their families behind, working couples—in fact, all whose needs did not rate larger living units. Their often attractive common rooms provided space for dorm parties, a definite feature of the Project's social life. The center of Los Alamos, its raison d'être, was of course the Tech

Scattered over the whole site were dormitories. . . . They housed single people, married people who had left their families behind, working couples—in fact, all whose needs did not rate larger living units. Their often attractive common rooms provided space for dorm parties, a definite feature of the Project's social life. (Los Alamos Historical Museum)

Area. About that I can say nothing, never having been beyond the wire fence. However, from a purely geographical point of view, one might say that Los Alamos centered about the Commissary and the old buildings which once composed Los Alamos Ranch School. The old buildings, now known as Fuller Lodge and Big House, and the few permanent houses which made up Bathtub Row were built before the frantic haste of wartime forced a mushroomlike crop all over the mesa; they were constructed, not of plywood or wallboard, but of logs and stone. They were not all of the same pattern, and they had grass and flowers around them—the result, no doubt, of much labor—but oh, how thrilling to see them there! My three-year-old son, after having lived in Los Alamos for two or three months, said one day, "I want to see a tree with leaves. I'm tired of pine needles." The implied complete lack was perhaps exaggerated, but it was near enough to the truth for me to sympathize with him, so we walked over to see these older buildings and, more particularly, the "trees with leaves" around them.

It was so, also, with other things we missed. For instance, after months of performing my ablutions under a shower, it was pleasant indeed to go into one of these permanent houses and refresh my memory as to the form and color and general aspect of a bathtub.

The buildings originally planned to serve as housing were of two types: one-story buildings containing two apartments and two-story buildings containing four apartments. These buildings dominated the scene in Los Alamos. They were painted green, and even though the shade varied a little according to the house's vintage, the greenness remained unrelieved. The small (one-story) two-family green houses were, in my estimation, the most attractive type on the mesa. For one thing their sloped roofs gave them a certain distinction among Los Alamos buildings; for another, in contrast with the larger green houses, they needed no outside staircases. Housing only two families, they also did not display such large quantities of laundry as usually festooned the four-family houses. These larger houses were flatly, uncompromisingly rectangular, and the net result was a large green block. The net result of several together was such an amazing mixture of quick glimpses of attractive interiors and extremely full views of repellent exteriors with masses of coal bins, wood piles, back stairs, and garbage pails that my reaction to it all tended to be subjective, dwelling on either the pleasantness within or the unpleasantness without, according to my mood. The pleasantness within was almost axiomatic. It was the result of the presence of pleasant people. The unpleasantness immediately without was perhaps the inevitable result of building large-scale housing so quickly in so remote a spot. Nevertheless, accounting for the cause did not alleviate the situation. People who had returned to civilization after living in Los Alamos and who then visited it again seemed always to be surprised—they had forgotten that it was "so slummy looking."

Perhaps the thing which contributed most to the tenement atmosphere was a sound idea on the part of the town planners: they had built the houses with the backs to the roads. This enabled deliveries of everything from furniture to groceries to be made with as little difficulty as possible. From one's front door one could look across to someone else's front door, and those fortunate enough not to have another house blocking the view could look across pine trees to the Jemez Mountains. Of course it sometimes worked out that someone looked from his front door across to someone else's back door, for Los

They had built the houses with the backs to the road. . . . The idea was probably sound efficiency, but the effect on roads was to make them look more than a little back-alleyish. (Los Alamos Historical Museum)

Alamos roads were not laid out with the precision of a checkerboard. The idea was probably sound efficiency, but the effect on roads was to make them look more than a little back-alleyish. The backs of the houses were designed with porches upstairs and down connected by a stair-case, so that the railings traced a large capital Z the bottom of which was interrupted by the coal box, the woodpile, and the entrance to the furnace room. Washing was likely to be flopping in quantity on the porches and on lines beside the houses. The addition of a little chicken wire could make the porches baby-proof and almost always did, for in Los Alamos babies were produced in wholesale quantities.

Nowhere on the ground was there any sustained greenness. Whether out of nostalgia or just a dogged will to succeed, some people tried year after year to create gardens. They first carried up soil from the floor of some canyon and injected it into the yellow or gray dust beside their houses. Then by dint of much watering they sometimes achieved rows of green seedlings and occasionally knew the triumph of actually eating the fruits or, in this case, the vegetables of their labor. This was rare, however, and even these hardy souls did not attempt to create lawns; rather, they did not long persevere in such attempts. The only place I know of where grass was actually grown successfully enough to make a large patch of green was around the old permanent buildings. Even there, owing to the unwonted traffic over it, the grass appeared to be on the way down. Around most of the houses, although there might be jack pines and in summer an occasional hollyhock or vine of sweet peas, the color of the ground was the color of dust, dotted with clumps of tough grass and hardy weeds, which added an unkempt air to a picture already none too promising. For most people, the things that happened inside the houses were far more important than the outside appearance. After the first shock, we got used to it, and when we went outdoors we were conscious instead of the exuberant pervasive sunshine, the clear air, and the serene mountains in the distance.

For newcomers to Los Alamos, the immediate question was that of who got which house. The earliest comers tell hair-raising stories of how during the first weeks they slept more or less in layers on the floors of Fuller Lodge and the permanent houses, or of how they commuted twenty or thirty miles over unimproved New Mexico roads from ranches, inns, or whatever presented itself in the way of temporary accommodation. To these first-comers went the first houses as soon as they were completed. Even at the beginning houses seem to have been allotted and rent exacted on the interesting general principle of "to each according to his need and from each according to his salary." Apartments in the small green houses contained only one bedroom; in the large green houses, apartments had either two or three bedrooms. Even the Morgan and McKee houses, in spite of their initial impression of identical repetition, came in three sizes, with one, two, or three bedrooms.

The only way to obtain a three-bedroom house was to have enough family to fill one; it was assumed that no one would be so rash as to have enough family to fill more! Regardless of the sort of house one needed, the rent charged was always a percentage of one's salary.

It was an exciting experience, I thought, in the socialization of housing. It established a sort of basic equality and removed a source of unfruitful competition. Then I found that there were exceptions to these rules. At one end of the housing scale were the Bathtub Row houses, which were often roomier than the new housing. They were given to directors of various kinds, and when a vacancy occurred, duration of residence and size of family determined the next occupant. On at least one occasion, when three families found themselves equally qualified to fill a vacant Bathtub Row house, the matter was settled amicably by drawing lots. But there were only a few houses in Bathtub Row, and it was fair enough to give them to prominent people.

At the other end of the scale were the trailers; even in this ideally arranged setup, it seemed that there was after all some class discrimination. To the original small group of scientists Los Alamos had been pictured as a remote spot where they might work alone and without interruption. But as this work progressed and more and more machinists, carpenters, builders, and technicians, as well as more scientists, were needed, the housing was taxed to the limit and sometimes fell behind requirements. For this reason the houses proper were reserved for the scientists and for military people over a certain rank, and the machinists and carpenters were accommodated in the trailer area. As any broad rule tends to do, this one involved a certain amount of hardship for the people who had families and who remained on the site for extended periods. By and large, however, it was probably a fairly good solution, as many of these men came for limited periods to certain jobs, and salaries paid to them as a group were higher than those paid to the scientist group. Nowhere in Los Alamos were there so many *so* elegant cars as there were in the trailer areas.

Perhaps the most surprising thing about living in a Los Alamos house was the service we received. When the coal bin was empty, or often before, men appeared in a large truck to fill it up again. When the wood box was empty, it was promptly refilled. (All the green houses had fireplaces.) Most surprising of all was to have a man knock at one's door, saying that he had come to check the electrical connections and making solicitous inquiries about the state and number of one's electric light bulbs, or saying that he had come to check the plumbing and after an hour or so spent in examining pipes and drains announcing that new faucets were necessary in the kitchen and forthwith installing them. Late in the summer a carpenter would present himself, inquire about windows and doors, then repair doors which might have been refractory and apply weather stripping to drafty windows. Of course, there were times when every available pair of hands was busy in the

Tech Area and odd repairs were done by the occupant or, unless extremely urgent, not at all. Usually, however, for something requiring a repair job, one left a work order at the Housing Office, and in due time the job was taken care of.

It was to the Housing Office that we went when we wished to move. We had lived in our little McKee house for nearly six months, and with the coming of cold weather the children spent more time indoors, taxing the house's capacity almost to the bursting point. We wanted to move to a three-bedroom green house, the rooms of which were enough larger to justify the work of moving. The system of priority was observed and we waited our turn for the kind of house we wanted. When it came, we kept in touch through the Housing Office with the progress of the cleaners and with current estimates as to when it would be ready. For when a house was vacated and before it could be reoccupied, it was cleaned by a troupe of Spanish-Americans. Theoretically, this was always done. In practice, some notable lapses occurred when workmen were busy in the Tech Area, but on the whole the affair was pretty well run. True, the cleaning men sometimes did not seem to use every possible moment at their disposal. Nevertheless, everyone appreciated moving into a sparklingly clean house when the men had finished their job.

With each type of house went a standard allotment of GI furniture. It was not particularly beautiful, but it served its purpose. People who had brought no furniture with them could get along quite passably with the GI allotment, and those who had been wise enough or foolish enough to bring their own could use it to fill in gaps. Those with their own things had much the more attractive houses and no storage bills. On the other hand, many people had moved clear across the continent to reach Los Alamos, and some of them considered that, like moss on a stone, furniture remains at its best if undisturbed. Furniture could be scratched or broken in moving and, once in Los Alamos, chairs and tables commenced to dry out alarmingly.

We had to apply to the warehouse for furniture and to the Housing Office for most other things connected with the maintenance of houses. Sometimes the quantities of red tape we encountered gave us the feeling that we were contacting a mysterious set of subordinates whose first duty was to shield the higher authorities from any contact with the outside world. It was like living in the dream world of one of Kafka's novels. Take, for instance, the affair of the stove.

In due time, our house was ready and we moved—the Friday before Christmas. The process was simplified by the fact that the furniture remained behind. Soon we were in our new house.

The green houses originally were equipped with monstrous coal- and wood-burning cooking stoves popularly known as Black Beauties. As these houses also had all-too-efficient heating systems, the effect on the kitchen temperature when a Black Beauty was fired up can be left to the imagination. Many people, therefore, had had them removed, and they cooked instead with hot plates and small electric roasters. This was what our predecessors had done, and so in our new house there was no stove. At Christmas, I just had to have a stove, so I went to the Housing Office to phone the warehouse. Someone who, to judge by his voice, was enjoying Christmas a little in advance promised to send a stove, pronto. The afternoon passed; no stove appeared. I phoned again. This time, there arrived a spindly-legged, ovenless three-burner oil stove, which I promptly sent back. I phoned again (a third trip to the Housing Office) and the voice, even merrier and less coherent, promised me with all the solemnity it could muster that we should receive a stove with an oven the following day. The following day the warehouse was closed, the Housing Office was closed, and no stove appeared. Obviously it was time to act. We took matters into our own hands and quietly stole the kerosene stove from our McKee house. It rose to the occasion and cooked our Christmas dinner. The day after Christmas, I reported our theft to the warehouse, adding that we should be pleased to keep the stove in question. They were not sure about that—it was not according to precedent.

Later, when something was baking in the oven, along came a truck and some men who carried up a White Beauty—large and cumbersome, but much less offensive than the big black ones. My stove was hot, so they could not move it at the moment. Promising to return in the morning, they left the White Beauty on the porch. Morning came and so did the men. They proceeded to remove not my kerosene stove, but the White Beauty. They did not seem to know why. "Them's our orders, ma'am!" was the last we heard of the matter. We still have the kerosene stove. Kafka himself could do no better than that.

Life on the Project was always a trifle makeshift, but that life fostered a fine community spirit. People got along with incomplete supplies of many things. Going to a party, I might meet someone else arriving with a hot plate tucked under an arm or carrying an extra chair. Through it all, everyone worked at top speed, knowing that this sojourn at Los Alamos would last for the duration of the war, however long that might be. Still, in spite of the makeshift, in spite of limited space, in spite of back stairs and garbage pails, we all had houses to live in. That, during the stress of war, is a great deal.

JANE S. WILSON

Jane Wilson, who depicts the many and varied phases of life at Los Alamos, taught English in the Los Alamos High School. Her husband, Robert Wilson, directed experiments on the Los Alamos cyclotron and was Division Leader of Experimental Nuclear Physics. He then became an Associate Professor of Physics at Harvard University.

The Wilsons moved to Ithaca, New York, in 1947, where they remained for 20 years. While Robert directed the Laboratory of Nuclear Studies at Cornell University, Jane reared three sons and published many articles and book reviews. In 1967, the Wilsons moved to Chicago and then, when the site became available, to Batavia, Illinois, where Robert was the first Director of Fermi National Laboratory. For a number of years Jane was book editor for the "Bulletin of the Atomic Scientists." She also edited two books, *Alamogordo Plus Twenty-Five Years* (Viking Press, 1971) and *All in Our Time* (Bulletin of the Atomic Scientists, 1974, 1975). The Wilsons now live in Ithaca, New York.

4
NOT QUITE EDEN

Jane S. Wilson

Los Alamos was sometimes called Shangri-La. I suppose this designation referred to the secret quality of the place, the physical, spiritual, and psychological separation of our community from the rest of the world. Beyond that, it bore little resemblance to James Hilton's idyllic spot in the mountains of Tibet. In the mountains of New Mexico, the women aged. We aged from day to day. Our electric power was uncertain. Our water supply ran out. Crisis succeeded crisis. Everything went wrong. We had few of the conveniences which most of us had taken for granted in the past. No mailman, no milkman, no laundryman, no paper boy knocked at our doors. There were no telephones in our homes. We shared unique difficulties of living with our husbands without sharing the recompensing thrill or sometimes even the knowledge of the great scientific experiment which was in progress.

Even under these somewhat trying circumstances, we managed to maintain our good humor. There were compensations. For one thing, our husbands weren't in uniform and separated from us. The country around the site was magnificent. We found ourselves among a most congenial and interesting group of people. We women realized that we were part of something a great deal bigger than ourselves.

Los Alamos was unique, but not only because the town labored and brought forth an atomic bomb. That was noteworthy. The really marvelous thing was that we managed to adjust ourselves to the oddest conditions under which a community has ever been maintained and within these limits to lead reasonably normal, happy lives. We were a secret project, probably the most secret project which has ever existed in the United States. That one fact dominated our existence.

43

For months after our arrival in New Mexico we had no address. For almost two years we could travel only within a radius bounded on the north by Taos and on the south by Albuquerque. We led an ingrown social life because we could not visit our friends or family, we could not be visited, and we were forbidden to make new friends among the people of nearby communities. We lived night and day, year after year, behind a guarded fence. We had joined the Project with the understanding that eventually the gates were going to close behind us, and we would not even be able to go to Santa Fe for necessary shopping. We were ready for that contingency, although its psychological repercussions would have been enormous. I know that I thought of it with a sinking heart—no escape from the mesa, not even for a day! Fortunately, this threat never materialized, and after a time even the travel restrictions were relaxed.

The shadow of Security lay everywhere, however. The group of Army officers who were our G-2, our Intelligence, our guardians, were a kind of universal bogey. We wanted to cooperate with them, heaven knows, but often rules were contradictory or vague. Sometimes the restrictions seemed arbitrary. We felt that, atomic bomb or no atomic bomb, we were still free men and women, and we protested vigorously when a new law seemed stringent or unnecessary. Security occasionally issued pamphlets which were supposed to orient the utterances of the citizenry. They only confused me. "Don't mention the topographical details which are essential to the Project," one pamphlet warned us. "What details?" thought I, feeling like a child who has had one too many rides on a merry-go-round. Were the sunsets essential to the Project? Were the mountains? The canyons? The result of Security's noncommittal policy was that for fear of saying the wrong thing, one said as little as possible. Letters home were inclined to be terse and in my case, anyhow, painfully self-conscious. I couldn't write a letter without seeing a censor pouring over it. I couldn't go to Santa Fe without being aware of hidden eyes upon me, watching, waiting to pounce on that inevitable misstep. It wasn't a pleasant feeling.

Once, by chance, I met an acquaintance from my college days on the streets of Santa Fe. It had been more than a year since I had talked to anyone I knew other than the people who lived on the Hill. It was wonderfully exhilarating to see someone from the outside world, someone whose life wasn't all mixed up with supersecret matters. But even this encounter was against the rules.

"Come have a Coke with me," my friend suggested, little realizing the enormity of her proposition.

I was numb with embarrassment. Woodenly, I accepted the invitation, although my conversation was a succession of fluid grunts. A moment's slip and I, by nature blabbermouthed, felt that I would find myself hurtling into the gaping entrance to hell. It was a relief to say goodbye. Then, like a child confessing that she has been naughty, I reported my social engagement to the Security Officer. Everything had to be reported to the Security Officer. Living at Los Alamos was something like living in jail.

Because any representative listing of Project personnel would have revealed a suspicious concentration of nuclear physicists, such lists were forbidden. For this reason, we were prohibited from depositing money in Santa Fe, and all our banking was done by mail. Automobile licenses and New Mexico state income taxes were made out to numbers rather than to names. Drivers' licenses were also anonymous. As far as the New Mexico records were concerned, one was driver 66 or driver 23. Later, when the war was over and my husband tried to sell his car in California, he was hamstrung as a result of such practices. He found he couldn't transfer the title to the car, because he didn't have it. He was shown to the door, babbling "atomic bomb" in vain.

Our mail was censored. Furthermore, our correspondents were not supposed to know that it was censored. The method was simple. Mail went into the box unsealed, the censor read it, sealed it, and sent it on its way. Or, if he didn't approve of the letter, he sent it back. Sometimes this system proved useful. If one of us intended to send a letter with an enclosure, such as a check, and then forgot to enclose it, the letter would come back with a note from the censor politely chiding the sender for his absent-mindedness.

I can't vouch for the authenticity of my favorite censor story, which concerns a letter written by a chemist about the trials of his particular job. "I wish that I had spent more time on dramatics at school," he wrote wistfully. "I certainly have a bunch of prima donnas to manage here!" The censor returned the epistle with a note pointing out that the writer was forbidden to reveal the nature of his work.

Innocent correspondence was often suspect for one reason or another. A young theoretical physicist whose wife was desperately ill in a sanitorium sought to divert her by writing her letters in code. The censor didn't like this. A student in the high school, writing about her studies to a girlfriend, illustrated her discussion of elementary biology with some sketches of amoeba walking. This was returned by the censor, who doubtless realized that amoeba don't walk—they reproduce by fission!

Everyone at Los Alamos accepted the fact that Security was necessary if our Project were to succeed. Many of us had been primed, before we arrived, for a much more stringent supervision. We had called it the "Concentration Camp Project" and were therefore quite pleased with whatever freedoms we were allowed. In the very early days of the Project, by our own rules, no one could mention the professions "physicist" and "chemist" even within the gates. We called them, I'm sorry to admit, "fizzlers" and "stinkers." A friend in the Tech Area, seeking the Chemistry Office, once asked a janitor, "Where is the Stinker's Office located?" He led her up the stairs and down a long hallway, then ceremoniously opened a door and ushered her in. She was embarrassed to find herself in the Ladies Room.

Security was more professional than this, and while it indulged in code words, they were never such childish ones. True, Security was almost always inconsistent, often high-handed, and sometimes unjust. As a group, we civilians disliked the Security Office, for it isn't a pleasant or easy thing to surrender one's rights as an American citizen. I dare say the feeling was reciprocal. Security had an ugly, thankless job to do in the face of great difficulties, and it seems to have done its job well.

Even if Security had not been breathing down our necks, life at Los Alamos would have been unusual, if only because of our physical isolation. The only way that many of us could get to the "mainland" of Santa Fe was by a free bus operating at rather inconvenient hours. The bus drivers had evidently been selected on the criterion of sociability. As the bus plowed down the hairpin turns of our mesa into the New Mexico desert, I found it disconcerting to have the driver swivel around for a little chat with a passenger. I couldn't forget the number of cars that had already plummeted down the steep cliffs and I never enjoyed these rides.

The bus was the least of our worries. Because Los Alamos was so far from the railroad tracks and busy markets of civilization, because it had been built in a great hurry, without much planning and with some inefficiency, it was scarcely an Eden. Consider the houses: even though four walls and a roof have since become a commodity more precious than rubies, I still cannot recall our living quarters at Los Alamos with affection. The rough woodwork and warped flooring of my duplex constituted a monument to poor workmanship. The building chanced to have an excellent location, set off by itself instead of being regimented into a row of similar buildings. The house was surrounded by pine trees spared through some miracle from the Army's ubiquitous axe. My husband and I were on the site when our house was being erected and, being new and innocent regarding the inflexibility of military regulations, the two of us tussled on several occasions with something the workmen called The Contract. The Wilsons always lost.

"Please don't paint the fireplace," we begged. "We want those fine red bricks to show. Besides, you'll save paint and labor."

"We can't do that," replied the inexorable foreman. "Why, The Contract calls for painting the fireplace!" And the fireplace was painted.

The Contract also included the installation of a wooden table and built-in benches in the kitchen. We didn't want them. We had our own kitchen table and chairs. My husband and I went to the foreman of the construction gang. "Don't bother putting in the table and benches," we said with our most winning smiles. "We'll only take them out again."

Just to be on the safe side, we plastered our tiny kitchen with warning notes: "No table and benches, please!" But the contractor's men could be halted no more than the flood of the Sorcerer's Apprentice. One morning, while both my husband and I were away at work, the genii of The Contract sneaked into our apartment, pushed our own kitchen table and chairs carefully out of the only nook available for them, and fulfilled their destiny. In went the table, in went the benches—but the workmen were kind. The nails had been barely tapped into the wall, and it was a simple matter to rip out the furniture we had to have because The Contract called for it.

Even before we moved into our apartment, my husband declared that the furnaces were much too big for the houses they heated. When winter came, I discovered how right he was; one hundred degree temperatures were not uncommon. I frequently came home to find that my candles had wilted and dripped out their lives over the floor. The original thermostat controlling the heat didn't work, and it was presently replaced by a more elaborate and expensive thermostat, which also didn't work. Even as the process of replacement was going on, thermostats of the first type were being installed in the new buildings under construction. After all, The Contract called for them!

Such inefficiency incensed me. As a taxpayer, I objected! My husband said that I had no sense of humor.

The heat which poured out of the grilled transoms in our walls left behind it a black and sticky trail of soot. The grime fell like gentle rain from heaven upon our walls, draperies, and furniture. Thus, despite a steady stream of Indian maids, my house could never be truly clean. The open transom was not only a purveyor of soot, it also carried voices distinctly from the furnace room. In winter, the furnace men would huddle there, often with a bottle, and have excited arguments in the Spanish patois which is the only language most of them know. These disembodied voices would make it almost impossible to conduct a conversation within the house. The result was a curious lack of privacy. Sometimes the furnace men didn't speak, but lustily raised their voices in song. They seemed in remarkably good voice, at that.

In winter, soot poured through the transoms. In summer, dust poured through the doors and windows. Too many trees had been chopped down by the Army. Construction was always in progress and this, in league with the region's natural aridness, created a dust situation the like of which I had not experienced before. One's home and one's person were always garden plots, God wot! I would not have been surprised had potatoes sprouted in my scalp.

The military administration, with what struck me as typical perversity, had given each apartment a splendid modern electric refrigerator with one hand and a hideous, curvaceous, very bleak wood- and coal-burning range with the other. One frightened look at this item, familiarly known as the Black Beauty, and I was in tears. Eventually, to supplement this monster, we were issued hot plates. I did all my cooking on two hot plates plus my own electric broiler and electric roaster. With such implements, I would nonchalantly whip up dinner, occasionally for as many as thirty-five. This was difficult but not impossible, except when the power was shut off. There were periods when this happened frequently, sometimes for hours at a time. If dinner happened to be ready, we ate by candlelight. If our meal was not yet cooked, occasionally we did not eat at all.

Graver than the uncertainty of the power supply was the water shortage. The Jemez is a dry land. One can scour the country for miles around and glimpse no body of water save green pools of sour sewage.

One of the first headaches of the administration, then, was obtaining a water supply adequate for the needs of the expanding community. After three and a half years, that particular migraine remains.

Our water, squeezed from suspect and distant sources, could not be considered pure and undefiled. Even when the town was small, typhoid shots were strongly recommended. Sometimes it seemed a formalism to call the fluid water, for our pipes apparently yielded unadulterated chlorine. The soldier entrusted with the task of purification set about his job with so much enthusiasm that he was soon in bed with chlorine poisoning. Still, we were informed, there was a water shortage. We found that strange since none of us was drinking water. We had turned to less pungent thirst quenchers.

As more and more people arrived to work on the Project, the water shortage grew acute to the point of hysteria. Soldiers leaped out of jeeps to present the latest bulletins on the water crisis to anxious householders. As I remember these documents, they were compendiums of fascinating facts and figures. A shower turned on full force for ten minutes would use so many gallons, the bulletins informed us. A Good Citizen's Shower, the merest trickle of spray lasting a minute or two, just time for the chorus of an aria, would use so many fewer gallons. The bulletins contained other angles for water conservation. Leaking faucets should be reported immediately. Watering of lawns or gardens was forbidden. Bodies should be soaped before entering the shower, a ceremony which could be disastrous if the water didn't come on. Toilet bowls should not be flushed in play.

This first water shortage occurred during the summer of 1943, the year the Project began. Crises of a similar nature followed throughout 1944. In 1945, the ominous rumblings about drought grew louder and more frequent. Charts were posted to prove that the supply simply couldn't keep up with the demand. I was inured to water scares by this time. When the faucet dripped, I was insouciant and even got a slight thrill out of the sound. That summer, the bomb test in the southern part of the state was successful. Atomic bombs had been dropped on Hiroshima and Nagasaki. What had we to fear? Los Alamos was a town of triumph, and the carefree sound of flushing toilets rang out into the night.

Abruptly, then, the long-heralded blow fell. In the week before Christmas, just when holiday preparations were at their peak, the water was shut off. Parties were cancelled because hostesses had no clean plates. The rudest thing one could do was to use the bathroom in another house. Diapers went unwashed, and the town plunged into a grim and gray period of mourning.

After a day or two, a mimeographed circular arrived at my door. Water, it informed me cheerily, was now available in trucks in front of the hospital. Aforementioned water was of two types: (a) potable and (b) nonpotable. The latter, the circular insinuated slyly, was for flushing toilets. This, by way of bucket, is something of a fine art, incidentally. Now all I had to do was to furnish my own containers and lug the water away. The circular suggested that I keep my vessels for (a) potable and (b) nonpotable water separate and distinct. Then, rather unnecessarily I thought, since there was not a drop of water in the house, it added the stern admonition that bathing was strictly prohibited except in cases of emergency. What such cases might be, it did not deign to say.

Gradually the situation became somewhat alleviated. Water managed to struggle through the taps for about an hour every day. This was the time frantically to fill pails and basins of all description with the brown liquid, heavy with sediment. Upon at least two occasions, I found vermillion worms swimming in my treasured supply. The water was ice cold and I wouldn't sit in it myself. In fact, personal cleanliness by now was in such a state that I avoided social gatherings. During this difficult period, I was heartened by a bulletin signed by the chief Los Alamos doctor. This leaflet stated that the current rumor about the hospital's being choked with typhoid patients was a malicious falsehood, but it asked sternly, "Have you had your typhoid shot yet?"

Although we had anticipated epidemics, they didn't materialize— except for the omnipresent "itis" (more succinctly known as the trots) and the usual children's diseases. Robert Oppenheimer, Director of the Project, had chicken pox accompanied by 104 degrees of fever. One can't shave when one has chicken pox. Our thin, ascetic Director looked like a 15th-century portrait of a saint with his fever-stricken eyes peering out from a face checkered with red patches and covered by a straggling beard. The school was once closed for a week because of a polio scare. Our many and various canine citizens were confined to their homes for a period when hydrophobia was suspected to be among us. No one died of polio or rabies, but the way panic filtered through the entire population was interesting to observe. We were on the *qui vive* for anything and everything. Ordinary day-by-day living had the intensity and unreality of a restless dream.

Several anecdotes illustrate how we people of Los Alamos went through the looking glass into a wonderland far beyond even Alice's imagination. They are not hilariously funny stories, but they represent the way that SNAFU might well have been our password and our slogan.

A car belonging to a neighbor was stolen from the front of his house. It seemed an easy matter to follow the car's movements because all cars going out of the gate had their license plates meticulously checked and jotted down by the guard on duty. If the car was still on the Hill, it should be easy to find for we had enough Military Police on the site to provide law enforcement officers for a community ten times the size of Los Alamos. Here was an opportunity to test their mettle. My neighbor discovered that on one of the few occasions when the list of vehicles leaving the site would have been valuable, those careful notations had been most carelessly lost. The missing car was eventually found directly behind MP headquarters, exactly where some joy-riding youngster had parked it *three* weeks before.

It was one of the rules that all our guns and cameras be checked in the Army vault, and we were given receipts for them. When my husband and I were leaving Los Alamos, I went to the vault to collect our property, a shotgun and a Brownie camera. After I had waited an hour for the sergeant who was responsible for the vault, he finally made an appearance. He looked at my receipts, perplexed. "This is the old kind," he said, accusingly.

"We are old residents," I replied.

He took me into the vault with him. "Look, lady, I might as well tell you that I have absolutely no way of figuring out which gun and which camera are yours. I tell you what, you just pick out any Brownie that looks good to you."

I rescued my husband's gun, which during its years in the safe deposit had unaccountably lost a piece off its stock. I followed the soldier's advice and picked out a Brownie that looked good to me. It wasn't mine. As I departed, the soldier said, "There'll be a day of reckoning soon." I agreed with him.

This was Los Alamos, then. It was a Barnum and Bailey world. We citizens loved it. Our hardships were pretty petty. We were animated by a drive to finish a vast and awful task. Compensation for Security, the water shortage, and all the rest of our ordeals lay with the people who shared them with us. They were the great, the near-great, the have-to-be-great. They were our friends and neighbors. Their person-alities made Los Alamos the wonderful experience it was.

I find a misapprehension about scientists in current newspaper sto-ries about them. "So and so," says a newspaper reporter in surprise, "does not look like a typical scientist." Had the reporter lived at Los Alamos for a while, he would have realized that there simply aren't any typical scientists, that an almost flamboyant individualism is the rule among us. The people on the Hill were tolerant of idiosyncrasy. We were, if anything, proud of the fact that in science one need not conform to a pattern of dress or behavior in order to succeed.

I would have been happy to conduct a journalist down the dusty roads of Los Alamos while he sought that stereotype of his, the typical scientist. The scene, at six o'clock on a late summer's day, might have looked like this:

The men are drifting home from the Tech Area. The sun slants down on the mountains, and the pine trees which line the road whisper in the breeze. A man and his wife hustle into a car loaded with saddles and Navajo blankets, off to locate their horses for an evening's ride. This scientist's hobby happens to be philosophy, but he is not very good at it. For the past five years he has been carefully reading William James. He is an excellent rider, however, and has a passion for parlor games, particularly "The Game." Is he typical?

Down the road a bit, a great bruiser of a physicist, stripped to the waist, is swinging dumbbells in his back yard. On the stoop sits his wife, who reads him choice bits from the latest *Wall Street Journal.* Perhaps a little later he will go into the house for a hearty swig of cod liver oil and then attempt to telegraph his broker.

His next-door neighbor, a gangling Englishman, is preparing for his fifth venture into the mountains to shoot a bear. The desire to take a bear skin back to Oxford has become the consuming ambition of his life. There are few wild animals on the dry slopes of the Jemez Moun-tains. No one that I know has ever seen a bear there. But the English physicist's enthusiasm is undampened, and he keeps hoping.

Strolling around Ashley Pond come three portly gentlemen. They look something like the journalist's typical scientist, for they have a wild and distracted air. All three are speaking at once; their faces are grave, and their eyes sweep the ground as if it held the answer to all enigmas of the universe. Perhaps they *are* discussing relativity. But I have overheard this trio on many similar occasions and suspect that it is more likely they are talking about John Von Neumann's classic theory on how to win at poker.

The only thing typical about the men of science at Los Alamos was that they were atypical, brilliant in a particular field, perhaps, but interested in diverse fields. Living among them would not have been such fun had many of them not been a little peculiar.

One thing quite characteristic of the scientists at Los Alamos was their youth. Gray hairs were rare among us. Many laboratory workers had interrupted their studies at universities to come to the Project, and keeping these eligible young men out of a 1A draft classification was a Project headache. Joe Kennedy, division leader in Chemistry, was twenty-eight years old. Another division leader was only thirty-one. Robert Oppenheimer celebrated his fortieth birthday at Los Alamos. At twenty-seven, I felt comfortably middle-aged. A friend in her early forties told me the other day how shocked she was when she returned home and attended a faculty tea. "Why, I wasn't the oldest woman in the room by a long shot!" she said gleefully.

There were a great many foreigners on the mesa. The British Mission arrived in the summer of 1944, and there were some Englishmen among them. There were also Poles, Swiss, Canadians, Germans, and Austrians. Rudolf Peierls, a native of Posen, headed the delegation. His wife, Eugenia, had been born in Leningrad. Their life together had followed the pattern of many of the European scientists: they had traveled about the Continent, jobless, insecure, but undaunted. Finally, they settled in England, where their children were born. Then the blitz came. "What chance had my kids if the Nazis invaded?" Eugenia once asked me bitterly. "My poor Jewish children with their Russian mother!" So her babies of four and six years were packed off to Canada, and the Peierls family was not reunited for four long years.

Indeed, if any American on the Project had been unaware of the tragedy and horror that Fascism brings to the individual, he would certainly have learned a lesson from the life histories of the European scientists. Exile, poverty, persecution, the concentration camp, and vicious death for their dear ones—our European friends had seen them all. A Polish scientist on the Hill did not know for at least four years whether his wife and children, left behind on the bloody soil of his homeland, were dead or alive. I don't think he knows yet. An English physicist at Los Alamos lost his wife as the result of a German bombing raid. The war would come very close to an American even if he were on top of a mesa in New Mexico when his host, listening to a radio broadcast on fighting in Hungary, said simply, "My family is there."

There is considerably more laughter than tears in the stories about the personalities on the Hill. For security, the most famous scientists traveled under assumed names and had military bodyguards. Niels Bohr, despite a heavy Danish accent, was officially "Nicholas Baker." His mathematician son, Aage, who always came with him, was called "Jim." Bohr is universally adored, not only because he is a great scientist, but also because he is a great man. There was always considerable flurry when "Uncle Nick," as we affectionately called him, came for a visit. Naturally, the anglicized names occasioned a great deal of mirth among those in the know. We like to tell the story of Niels Bohr in a Washington elevator. Meeting a young woman who had recently married, he tipped his hat and said, "Pardon me. Aren't you Miss Smith?"

"No, I'm Mrs. Johnston," she replied. "But say, aren't you Niels Bohr?"

"Oh, no," murmured the father of the quantum theory. "I'm Nicholas Baker."

When Laura Fermi arrived in New Mexico, she and her children were almost stranded at the Lamy station. The Wac driver was looking for a Mrs. Henry Farmer. Mrs. Fermi, uninstructed regarding her new cognomen, had a hard time convincing the Wac that even if she wasn't the important Mrs. Farmer she should be driven to Los Alamos anyway.

We also like to tell the story, doubtless apochryphal, about the time the film "Madame Curie" was being shown at the Los Alamos theaters. According to that yarn, "Mr. Farmer" approached "Mr. Baker." "I've just seen a grand picture," he announced smugly, "Madame Cooper."

One of my favorite Bohr anecdotes, and a true one, concerns the early war years when nuclear energy was still a dream. Bohr, who had escaped from his native Denmark to Sweden, learned that the British scientists were beginning to investigate the possibility of an atomic bomb. He had an idea for an approach which might prove fruitful, and he sent to England a cryptic message saying, in part, "Notify Maud re Kent." This, obviously, was an important clue—a truly great mind was trying to help. For days the English scientists struggled to decode the memo, but in vain. For a long time the atomic bomb project, both in England and in America, was called the "Maud Project" in memory of this failure. Later, when Bohr came to Los Alamos, one of the first things he was asked was the key to his cryptogram. What had he meant in that urgent note, "Notify Maud re Kent"? Bohr offered apologies. Yes, that had certainly been one pip of an idea. Unfortunately, he no longer remembered just what it was.

Bohr was not the only absent-minded professor on the Hill. We loved the stories which were circulated about the people we knew. Sitting around our firesides in the evening, we spoke of the things which made up our life—the shortages, the difficulties, the personalities. The smallest details seemed important at Los Alamos. We lived intensely. It wasn't, of course, Shangri-La living, not at all. We were constantly annoyed by inefficiency and stupidity. There was nothing simple or easy about running a household on that secret mesa. But we could face it, aware of the drama of our situation, supported by the friends who lived so near to us, and finally, buoyed up by the fact that here at Los Alamos, an event of magnitude was being wrought.

CHARLOTTE SERBER

Charlotte Serber was one of the few women at Los Alamos who held an important position in the Technical Area. As Scientific Librarian she was in charge not only of reference books but also top-secret documents concerning the work being done. She and her husband, Robert Serber, joined the Project at its inception and were among the first people to arrive at Los Alamos. Dr. Serber was a Group Leader in the Theoretical Physics Division at Los Alamos and then a Professor of Physics at the University of California at Berkeley.

The Serbers lived in Berkeley from 1946 until 1951, when they moved to New York. There, Dr. Serber joined the faculty of Columbia University and Charlotte became a Production Assistant in the Broadway theater. She died in 1967.

5
LABOR PAINS

Charlotte Serber

The first look was always disappointing. The inside of the Tech Area was not that mysterious labyrinth of glamorous laboratories and offices which one had expected. The laboratories had a cluttered, disorderly, academic air. The offices were simple enough, though incredibly dirty, overcrowded, and badly equipped. Physically, the Tech Area was certainly not a very unusual place. But it did have a spirit which was strange. Its tempo was too fast; its excitement was almost too high. The Area was in a state of continuous crisis, and it soon became clear that speedup was its permanent tempo and excitement its permanent mood. This hyperthyroid quality was contagious and soon, in each newcomer to the Area, any disappointment with its physical drabness was rapidly followed by a real enthusiasm for both its work and its personnel.

In the early days of the Project, most of the women who worked in the Area were wives of young physicists and chemists. In a great many cases, they had not intended to work when they came to Los Alamos. But the force of social pressure and the obvious need for all hands, trained or untrained, brought most of them rapidly onto the payroll. They came mostly as secretaries, typists, or clerks. Some came as technicians, librarians, computors, or draftsmen, and a very few as scientists. They came intending to work only part time, but worked full time. They came intending to quit in a few months, but worked for a year or two. A very few came to do a specific job and worked until their husbands left the Project.

It is quite an experience, after all, to be an integral part of a top-

Physically, the Tech Area was certainly not a very unusual place. But it did have a spirit which was strange. . . . The Area was in a state of continuous crisis, and it soon became clear that speedup was its permanent tempo and excitement its permanent mood. (Los Alamos National Laboratory)

secret Project with an Army X-priority, particularly when you find yourself working side by side with the top-flight scientists of the world. Even those who did not know the nature of the problem or the reason for the secrecy seemed to catch a sense of the work's urgency and a feeling for its importance. The press of work was terrific at times, but there were many factors which eased it—the informality in the offices, the lack of office taboos, and the casualness of dress. The strange feeling of complete isolation from the world was somewhat compensated for by the people with whom one worked. They were unusual people. It was a unique job. The whole Project was radically different from anything one had ever met before, however one looked at it.

For those who came to Los Alamos at its inception, March 1943, the surprises and disappointments were even sharper. When the first hundred or so scientists and their wives arrived, they met endless unexpected situations and hardships. Everything was makeshift. Los Alamos was in no way ready to receive them. The housing had not been completed. The fence around the Post was half-finished. The Tech Area was an empty shell without power, gas, telephone, furniture, or equipment, and it was separated from the Post proper only by fence posts. To top it off, the MP detachment of guards had not arrived! Something drastic had to be arranged in a hurry. An office was set up in Santa Fe at 109 East Palace. Local Spanish-Americans were hired as guards. A few guest ranches outside of Santa Fe were taken over, since Security forbade people to register in Santa Fe hotels, and our personal cars were commandeered to run as buses to the site from these ranches. Lastly, everyone was put to work, usually at unfamiliar jobs such as rigging, teamstering, chauffeuring, and clerking. I had been hired on the Project as the Scientific Librarian, but since no books or reports had arrived yet, I also did another job. For the first month or two, I worked in the Director's Office, helping Priscilla Greene, the Executive Secretary.

Although the arrangement was awkward, certainly, the main office had to be in Santa Fe until a direct phone line was strung between it and Los Alamos. The only existing connection with the Hill was a ranger's telephone, a primitive crank affair. The telephone line, made of iron wire, lay directly on the ground and picked up endless static over the thirty-five miles between Santa Fe and the Hill. Life probably would have been simpler if that line had never existed for we did attempt to use it at times. Once a call came from the Hill asking us to send up eight extra lunch boxes. The request as we heard it above the noise, but lucidly could not fill, was for eight extra-large trucks.

The pass system of those early days was our own doing and showed the fine civilian hand of amateurs. Instead of simple cards or badges, our passes were typewritten letters on full-size heavy bond paper with three onionskin carbons, each copy personally signed by the Director. Truck drivers with a single load, as well as the regular staff, all had to have these. They were a nuisance to type since no erasures were allowed, and the system resulted in writer's cramp for the Director, bad tempers for the typists, and after a few days of use, a collection of the most bedraggled passes ever presented at an Army Post.

The mail was another headache. Security was very tight in the beginning, and as a result, the mail could not be handled in a normal fashion. We were instructed to tell our families, employers, and as few others as necessary that we were leaving for work on an Army Post, destination not revealable, and that our mail should continue to be addressed to our previous universities. At each of these institutions, one secretary was entrusted with the Santa Fe Post Office box number and she forwarded our mail in large bundles. In return, we pouched our outgoing mail and sent it to these same secretaries for remailing. I thoroughly confused my family by sending my letters home in different pouches so that one week they would get a Princeton postmark and the next perhaps a Berkeley one.

It was not until the telephone line was in and we actually moved the Director's Office to the Hill that the real circus over mail began. The wife of one of the chemists was shanghaied into the miserable job of mailman before she had been in Santa Fe five minutes and before she had even seen Los Alamos. Twice a day, every day, she went to Santa Fe in a broken-down car over a dusty, bumpy road, accompanied by an armed Spanish-American guard, to get the mail. She placed the registered mail in a locked briefcase, which in turn was locked to her wrist. I alone had the key. She invariably arrived on the Hill, breathless, just at lunch and dinner times, and would get me to unfetter her. Then there was no peace for me unless I immediately gave out the personal mail to everyone in the dining room.

After the telephone, pass, and mail problems had been "solved" in this fashion, Priscilla and I tackled the problem of stationery stock. We managed to purchase a mimeograph machine locally, but we so befuddled the storekeeper by our general confusion and the startlingly obvious fact that we knew practically nothing about mimeograph machines, that he forgot to get a War Production Board priority from us (which of course we did not have). Typewriters were harder to come by, but we managed to borrow a few from Santa Fe schools and charitable institutions. Luckily an Army shipment arrived a few days before we moved to the Hill.

The telephone was still a problem when we moved up. Along with the instruments, there also was installed in the Tech Area a small PBX switchboard, but no one knew how to run it. We got a quick lesson from the telephone company and then proceeded to shanghai and "train in" a number of working wives. In this way we kept the PBX going on an hourly, volunteer basis both day and night. The telephone was almost my nemesis. For the first two weeks after installation, there were no lightning arresters. One fine April afternoon a violent mountain thunderstorm came up. The telephone rang, and just as I was reaching for it, a bolt hit the line, traveled down it, and then sparked to the lamp cord just two inches from my hand. It blew out the lamp but not the telephone. For the rest of that day, however, few in the Tech Area were brave enough to answer the phone.

When the public-address system was installed, our favorite PBX operator happened to be on, and she christened the machine in dulcet tones, "At the sound of the gong, it will be 5:30. Everyone please go home." In about its second week of infancy, we still treated the PA as a fancy toy, serenading one of the senior scientists with "Happy Birthday." Such frivolous behavior was officially discouraged, but nevertheless practical jokes on the PA continued to crop up at times.

There was the time when the Tech Area was not developed beyond buildings called T, U, V, W, X, Y, and Z, and the PA operator announced "Will all personnel in Building X go to a meeting in Building T? Will all personnel in X please go at once to T?" A few minutes later, having been corrected by a humorist, she called "Correction please. Will all those in X please go to L?"

Another time, the operator, by request, insistently paged Werner Heisenberg at intervals for two days. Finally, a sympathetic soul took pity on her and explained that if she really wanted him she had better cable Berlin. Herr Heisenberg, the famous German physicist, was the director of the Nazi atomic bomb work.

Western Union really must have hated us. Our only means of sending or getting wires was via the telephone. There were wires in makeshift codes, wires that said only "Butane" or "Yes." There were wires in foreign languages. Wires and more wires. To this day, I have a tendency to spell out, before saying, such words as PHYSIKALISCHE ZEIT-SCHRIFT.

After a month on this most secret of secret projects, there were still no lockable files except the one in the Director's Office, which had been brought from Berkeley. This file became the combined storage warehouse and bank vault for the entire Project. Into it we crammed a potpourri of secret reports, confidential mail, precious platinum and gold foils, and even the cash of the staff members.

In those early days almost anything could happen, and it usually did. One April afternoon I was called into the Director's Office with physicist John Manley, the lieutenant in charge of G-2, and Priscilla. Dr. Oppenheimer told us that gossip in Santa Fe was becoming worrisome. He explained that rumors were getting wilder and wilder. They were saying that we were building a submarine for the Russians (on the driest mesa for miles!); they called Los Alamos a home for pregnant Wacs. It was funny, yes, but the worry was that sooner or later someone might guess a little closer to the truth. After all, a cyclotron had arrived by freight. To the public, cyclotrons meant University of California. University of California meant atom-smashing, and to someone, atom-smashing might mean atomic bomb. It therefore seemed expedient to spread a story in Santa Fe which was along scientific lines, was within the realm of possibility, and incidentally was incorrect. It had to account for all the civilian scientists, for the supersecrecy, and for the loud booms that Santa Feans were beginning to hear on fine mornings.

"Therefore," said Oppy, "for Santa Fe purposes, we are making an electric rocket."

This seemed like a fine idea to us, but it wasn't at all clear how we were to be involved since G-2 presumably could see that this story was spread. But then came the punch line.

Said Oppy, "I think that John and Charlotte can manage to get this story around. Go to Santa Fe as often as you can. Talk. Talk too much. Talk as if you had too many drinks. Get people to eavesdrop. Say a number of things about us that you are not supposed to. Say the place is growing. Finally, and I don't care how you manage it, say we are building an electric rocket. No one is to be told of this assignment. If you are successful, you will be reported on by G-2 in Santa Fe and by other Los Alamosites who overhear you. You will be protected if you get into trouble, but for the moment it is a secret mission."

Meekly, I asked if I could tell my husband, Bob, for how was I to explain many trips to Santa Fe with John? This seemed to make sense, so our "spy ring" was expanded to include Bob and Priscilla. We thus had a foursome for our expeditions to town.

Slightly bewildered, we left the office and made a date for that evening. The obvious place to go was the bar of La Fonda Hotel since it is a favorite with the local businessmen as well as with the tourist trade. We arrived there about 9 P.M. feeling a little silly and self-conscious. We found a table between two occupied ones and quietly ordered drinks. Our conversation was singularly dull as we each wondered how to bring electric rockets into it. We told little stories about Los Alamos, mentioning the forbidden name boldly and loudly. But no ears cocked in our direction; no one peered around at us. A few bored people quietly sipped their drinks and showed not the slightest interest.

After another round of drinks and no obvious sign that La Fonda business would pick up or wake up, we decided to try a less elegant bar. We might meet some construction laborers who worked on the Hill. They surely would be curious about what we were building and be anxious to learn our secret. To them, the people of Santa Fe, and not to the snobs and intellectuals, we would talk of electric rockets. We found a fairly crowded bar which sported a dance floor and were ushered to a booth. John and Priscilla got up soon, deciding that the dance floor might be a good place to be overheard. Instead of asking me to dance, Bob abandoned me without a word, went over to the most crowded part of the bar, and ordered himself another drink. No sooner had he gone than a young Spanish-American fellow, quite handsome, was bowing formally before me and requesting the honor of this dance. I recognized Bob's plan then, accepted with pleasure, and assumed my role of Mata Hari.

My innocent victim was solemn. He danced well and said nothing. I asked if he lived in Santa Fe.

"Yes."

I asked him what he did.

"Nothing."

"How come you're not in the service?"

"4F. Was working at Los Alamos, but I quit. Want to get a job on a ranch."

I was excited. The plan was working. This boy was familiar with Los Alamos and would certainly be curious. "We're up at Los Alamos now," I said.

"Uh-huh."

"It's quite a place, don't you think?" I persisted. "So mysterious and secret, and it seems to be growing by leaps and bounds. Notice all the different license plates?"

"Yeah. You know, I sure want to run a ranch someday. That's the only thing I want. . . ."

"But what do you suppose they're doing at Los Alamos?" I eagerly asked.

"I dunno. You sure dance fine. Hated working at that place. Didn't pay it no attention. Just want to get me a ranch and own some horses. Come to town often? You sure dance fine."

"We come to town as often as we can, but they don't like to let us out much. What's your guess about what cooks up there?"

"Beats me. Don't care. May I have another dance later?"

The dance ended and a rather dejected Mata Hari was graciously thanked and shown back to her table. John and Priscilla came back looking about the same. No one had listened to them. No one cared about the visitors from Los Alamos. But then Bob appeared. Bob, the quiet member of our group, who was only tolerated on this jaunt in order to avoid a family scandal, came back with success and smug self-satisfaction written all over his face.

We all asked at once, "Quick. What happened? Why are you so cheerful?"

It seems that he had gone up to the bar and landed next to a local rancher. He started a conversation like mine, and there was a similar lack of interest. However, instead of giving up, his story is that he practically took the man by his coat lapels, and said, "You know why they're making all those loud noises and explosions up there, don't you? They're tests. They're making electric rockets. That's what they're doing at Los Alamos." The rancher grunted and ordered another drink.

We gave up and started home. Bob was congratulated on his success, but in the car he confessed that the rancher had been so drunk he probably would not remember a thing when he woke up the next day. John and I decided to quit. We were obvious flops at building an electric rocket. Let G-2 work on that gadget. We would stick to the atomic bomb.

Our miserable failure at counterespionage soon was forgotten by Priscilla and me. There was still plenty to do. New arrivals were coming to the Project in droves, and they had to be given instructions, passes, housing, etc. We also had a heavy mail to answer from the scientists who were still not among us but who planned to be. We had to write and send out prospectuses that covered everything from the size of the bathrooms to the type of outdoor sports one might enjoy in New Mexico, Land of Enchantment, and we often sounded like a Chamber of Commerce. We had the regular scientific business that naturally emanated from the Director's Office. On top of all this we were beginning to show wear and tear, for we had been working seventy-hour weeks from February to May.

It was a big day when the first shipment of books for my library arrived. I was weary of hearing people remark, after looking around my barren shelves, "And in which section do you keep your detective stories?" I was really glad to see those books, as much as I hated leaving the nerve center of the Project. A few days later, a special courier arrived with several black suitcases crammed full of secret documents from other sections of the Manhattan District, and I finally moved from the Director's Office to the library. The bookshelves were there but the library vault was not finished, and finally an antique safe was located in which to temporarily store the secret reports. It had a unique combination, for although it was a three-tumbler affair, it required a swift kick at one crucial point or it refused to open. When I moved from second floor west to first floor east of the same building, Priscilla and I had a sad farewell. We made a pact to visit each other now and then. Little did we know that, with the expansion to come soon after, we were almost as close as two offices could be.

The Tech Area originally contained a group of buildings named T to Z, respectively, which housed the administrative offices, laboratories, library, warehouse, and shop. From this modest beginning, the place mushroomed into so many buildings that to name them we quickly ran through the English alphabet, moved into Greek and Hebrew, and finally into mathematical symbols.

The first buildings were drab and badly planned with soft, unvarnished floors, small windows, and poor incandescent lighting. Later, buildings varied from the elegant structure built for the chemists, which sported glass partitions, battleship linoleum, and an overabundance of fluorescent lighting, to the beaverboard chicken-coop built for the theoretical physicists.

Throughout the Project's existence, administrative rulings within the area were often confusing and inadequate. Up to the time I left the Project, there never was any official provision made for the disposal of waste paper upon which classified (secret, confidential, or restricted) material had been written. Although Security ruled that this paper must be burned, the actual burning was left to the discretion of the secretaries and scientists. Their discretion was often influenced by the discomfort of standing at an outdoor incinerator in below-freezing or blistering-hot weather.

Security ruled that all classified material must be locked up when not attended, but it established no controls. Finding ourselves an absentminded lot, we set up a policing system of our own. Nightly tours were made of the various offices to discover if any secret documents were carelessly left lying on a desk or in an unlocked file. If the inspectors tripped up a culprit, he could recover his offending document either by paying a stiff fine or by working off his punishment acting as an inspector himself for seven nights. These inspectors turned out to be the most efficient; they seemed to get a vicious delight in discovering another offender.

Even though we may remember a little bitterly these troubles and those we had over the lack of adequate janitorial service, office equipment, and messengers, I think we are more likely to remember the humor and friendship that was so basic to the work in the Area. At night, while some worked alone and quietly and others chatted and gossiped over a Coke, there seemed to be a pleasant calm, rarely achieved in the daytime. Soft music from a radio or phonograph often helped to create this quality of serenity.

In the daytime, even as some wrangled over who was going to get the newest typewriters or offices and others worried about much more serious problems, a light note would often ease the situation. There was the time one of the famous scientists refused to pay a fine for leaving a secret report on his desk overnight. His defense was that, since the report was completely wrong, not locking it up was commendable. Would it not confuse and mislead rather than aid and abet the nebulous enemy agent?

Physically and organizationally, the Tech Area certainly was a confusing place from its very beginning. It never achieved any real feeling of permanence and stability. It was a large, overgrown laboratory with many defects and gaps caused by its isolation and its mushroom growth. But one quickly adjusted to it. What is more important is that its purpose was clear throughout and therefore its remarkable tone remained intact, too. Until after Nagasaki, the Tech Area was a harried but exciting place in which to work.

Until we had a formal Personnel Office in full swing, most housewives were transformed into working wives by that mysterious chain reaction, the grapevine. Along the vine would come the word that someone was arriving the next day whose wife was a good secretary. Or, in reverse, the vine sometimes carried a message to a physicist that typists were needed, and he would ask if his wife could be of use.

For the working wife, the actual process of being hired in was not very complicated. It entailed filling in a multitude of forms, getting a pass to the Tech Area, listening to a speech on security, hearing an oversimplified version of working conditions on the Hill, and getting her salary set. Working conditions included forty-eight hours to the work week, two weeks of vacation with pay, sick leave, one day off a month for a shopping trip to Santa Fe, maids available through the Housing Office, and a nursery school for her children. The working wife's salary, which was set very arbitrarily, was influenced less by her previous work history than by the fact that she really had no bargaining power. She lived, after all, in a sort of company town.

For the potential working wife, there was one chief worry. Could she manage her home here on the mesa and work too? Would her home life suffer? Would her husband be neglected? Would her children become delinquents? Would it be any more difficult than working a forty-eight-hour week in a city?

On an Army Post, everyone always gripes. It is the convention. But looking at the problem as dispassionately as I can, I think that many of our problems were much simpler than those of our urban sisters. Shopping, for instance, was, in one sense at least, less complicated. There was only one Commissary. If it didn't have chicken, you couldn't waste time by going to another store. You simply forgot about chicken that night and ate pork or veal. If the laundry wasn't taking clothes one week, you were a little less fastidious or you did the washing youself at night. If there was no gasoline in the local tank, you walked to work. If the PX had no cigarettes, you rolled your own. Everything that did exist on the Hill was close by: Commissary, PX, trading post, dry cleaners, and beauty shop. And if what you needed could only be gotten in Santa Fe, you had a friend get it for you, or you waited until you could take a day off and get it yourself.

A trip to Santa Fe was a major event for working wives. Over a period of weeks, your list grew and grew. For some, the date for the trek was finally set by the state of their liquor supply; for others, by their supply of baby oil. When some such critical item hit bottom, your trip got classified ESSENTIAL. By this time, your list was long enough to consume three shopping days, but you always hopefully thought you could cover it. At the last minute, though, your chance slipped away. If you were going to town you looked different—a little more chic, perhaps a little gayer. If you wore a hat, it was a dead giveaway. Whatever it was, you were quickly noticed and besieged with requests for a great number of little items that "won't take a minute." Your list finally resembled the index of the Sears Roebuck catalog.

But off you went, and the morning in Santa Fe usually went well. You speedily got through the groceries, shoe repairs, toilet articles, and other straightforward items. You felt satisfied with the haul which half-filled the trunk of your car, so you had a pleasant leisurely lunch at La Fonda. But invariably you made the same mistake. You still had to cover the difficult items like clothing, furniture, and hardware. The afternoon was usually spent unsuccessfully, so about four o'clock you gave up completely, joined the other shop-weary Los Alamosites at La Fonda, and while quietly sipping a drink, rewrote most of your list for the next month's trip.

Although in some ways our problems may have been simpler than those of city wives, we never took them lightly. Take the question of domestic help. The amount of worrying and wrangling about this problem alone consumed almost as much gossiping time as the bomb itself. Like most things at Los Alamos, the history of domestic help dates back to the early days. Within about fifteen miles of Los Alamos there are three Indian pueblos, two towns, and a number of small farms, the closest being San Ildefonso Pueblo. In May 1943, the Security Office granted us permission to bring San Ildefonso women up to do housework for the working women. An Army carryall was to transport the original eight or ten Indians up to the Hill at 8:30 and down again at 5:30 each day. Except for this official help on transportation, the venture was a purely cooperative one, aided by a volunteer, non-working wife who made the schedules, met the bus, and assigned the women. Most of us got from three to six half-days of work a week and were delighted at this unexpected relief from housework.

As more and more people arrived on the Hill and because the press of work in the Tech Area never eased up, the demand for Indian maids grew tremendously. Nonworking women, coming late in the game, naturally expected and did get help. Working women wanted more help. The Housing Office finally took over the problem and, under the guidance of the Tech Area Personnel Office, set up a pseudo-Employment Office. It was a thankless job they inherited—rustling up new girls, getting everyone assigned, meeting demands, and settling arguments.

Slowly, the working women began to realize that this service was no longer run primarily for their benefit, but for the community as a whole, and that in a way they were losing ground. We had no time to haunt the Housing Office to ask special favors. In fact, we rarely had time to see our girls, relying on the Housing Office to send us girls who could follow our notes of instruction.

When demand got so far ahead of supply that things were thoroughly out of hand and hair-pulling arguments seemed a likely prospect, the Housing Office inaugurated a priority system. Illness and pregnancy were the highest caste, full-time working wives came next, then part-time working wives with children, nonworking wives with children, part-time working wives without children, and lastly, the nonworking, childless wives. A table worked out on the basis of the total number of available girls gave the maximum number of work days any member of each class could receive. At one point, when girls were so scarce that a further cut was imminent, the full-time workers were threatened with a maximum of two instead of our original six half-days a week.

A minor revolution brewed in our ranks. Finally, four of us stomped into the Personnel Office with an ultimatum. We really were threatening a strike, an unheard-of procedure at Los Alamos. We had a list of grievances and demands, and a deadline. The joker was that anyone knowing our quartet could call our bluff, and the personnel officer we went to see happened to know us all quite well. We had been on the Project from the early days, we all felt a personal responsibility for its success, and it would have taken a great deal more than this minor crisis to make us quit. Luckily for us, the officer met our demands and we never lost face.

The Indian girls were not always the cause of discontent and strife. Some of us got to know them a little and found them a charming, friendly group. At Christmas time, presents were always exchanged, and many of us have a fine collection of pottery as a result. We often got amusing notes from them. Once, when my husband was home ill in bed, I found this note on returning from work: "Mrs. Serber. I could not wash the sheets because your husband was in them. I will wash them tomorrow when I wash Mrs. Wilson. I am Josephine." So, our Josephines sometimes amused us, our Juanitas pleased us no end, and we worried ourselves over all of them. But in one sense we again were luckier than urban working wives. We at least always had some form and some amount of domestic help.

On the whole, the working wives managed their home economy fairly well. The question then arises, did we gain or lose anything by not being a part of the leisure class? What we gained, I think, is tremendous in a lasting way. To have been a working entity on the Project is something we don't forget easily. Even at the time, it was impressive. We were doing a war job in a period when people were needed badly. This was healthy and right. In addition, we happened to be part of a particularly spectacular project and we knew its day-to-day successes and failures. We also got to know a great number of people, fine people, from world-renowned scientists to buck-private would-be graduate students.

What, if anything, did we lose by working? We found that out one day when we called a meeting to nominate for the Town Council a working wife who would plug for our special interests. We discovered that we really had no special interests. Only one thing seemed to differentiate us from the other women. We had less time for shopping and for housework. Our meeting degenerated into a typical women's tea party with conversation centering on the scarcity of milk, the age of available eggs, and the wilted condition of the vegetables.

In retrospect, I can think of one trivial way we may have differed a little. I think, as a group, we looked different. First, we generally looked tired. Los Alamos had an active night life, and work began at 8:30 sharp. We never had enough sleep. Sunday, the day of rest, usually found us in conflict. The sensible thing to do was to sleep, but the country was so beautiful that it was hard not to ski, walk, ride, or fish as the season offered. Usually, Monday morning found us just as worn out as Saturday afternoon. Second, we dressed differently. We usually wore slacks, and sometimes jeans. We very often needed a shampoo. We weren't sloppy, really, but I am afraid we looked as if we dressed in a hurry, which we did.

A new arrival on the Hill was jostled out of his conventional idea of what a library staff is supposed to look like. Here, he was apt to find the librarian in blue jeans, one assistant in the best sweater-girl tradition, another in strict WAC uniform, and a third in the latest Lane Bryant number. The library was an odd place, anyway. It was the center for all gossip. It was a hangout. It had a document room and vault. It was the production center for all secret reports written on the Project. It was the sole owner of a ditto machine on which was run off everything from scientific reports to notices of ski club meetings. But it really was a library, too.

That was the thing about Los Alamos. It was anything but conventional. Everything was new and different and frantic. But we did a job and evidently did it well. History seems to have been written at Los Alamos, and I think the working wives can claim a small share of the writing.

—Alice Smith in 1963.

ALICE KIMBALL SMITH

Not only was Alice Smith a member of Town Council, she also taught history in the high school and administered to the needs of young Stuart and Anne. Her husband, Cyril Smith, was Associate Leader of the Chemistry-Metallurgy Division.

On January 1, 1946, the Smiths moved to Chicago where Cyril became Professor of Metallurgy and Founding Director of the Institute for the Study of Metals at the University of Chicago. Alice worked as Assistant Editor of the newly established "Bulletin of the Atomic Scientists." In September 1948 she became a Lecturer in History at Roosevelt College (now Roosevelt University), where she continued to teach English and European history until 1960. In 1958 the "Bulletin of the Atomic Scientists" published Alice's article on the wartime efforts of Chicago Met Lab scientists to avoid using the atomic bomb against Japan. The article became a book-length study of the scientists' postwar campaign for civilian and international control of atomic energy, *A Peril and a Hope* (University of Chicago Press, 1965; paperback MIT Press, 1970). In 1961 the Smiths moved to Cambridge where Cyril joined the Massachusetts Institute of Technology staff as Institute Professor. Alice completed *A Peril and a Hope* as a Fellow of the Radcliffe Institute (now the Mary I. Bunting Institute) and joined its staff in 1963, retiring as dean in 1973. She has published articles and read papers on the decision to use the bomb and on wartime Los Alamos. With Charles Weiner she co-edited *Robert Oppenheimer, Letters and Recollections* (Harvard University Press, 1980; papperback 1981).

6
LAW AND ORDER

Alice Kimball Smith

The Los Alamos Town Council was rather like a student government body. Its members might vote to abolish examinations, permit smoking in chapel, or move the college to New Haven, but political imagination was inhibited by the matter-of-fact attitude of faculty and administration.

So at Los Alamos. According to its bylaws, the Town Council had magnificent powers embodied in a kind of general welfare clause for the mesa, but its efforts were always circumscribed by the hard fact that we lived on an Army Post. However genuine the concern of the commanding officer for civilian comfort, orders from Washington determined how much each housing unit might cost, how many buses could take shoppers to Santa Fe, and how to deal in general with a queer assemblage of individuals who had their own code of discipline and asked for what they wanted as if they actually expected to get it.

The Council may not have represented the most lighthearted side of life at Los Alamos—the humor involved tended toward the ironic—but its three years of weekly minutes show a lot about us and how we lived, and how we grew from a small scientific community with a baby on every doorstep and a Beethoven concerto on every Victrola to a cross section of America. They show the reluctance of American civilians to take an iota more of minor regimentation than was absolutely necessary. One can interpret the griping that took place at Town Council week after week as a sign of the health of American democracy, or one may adopt the Army view that civilians are a cussed lot of humans anyway.

First, a word about government at Los Alamos. One of the oddest anomalies of our curiously anomalous life there was our judicial and political status. Once inside the Project fence we were outside the clutches of New Mexico law. We were strictly the responsibility of the Army, and yet we presented problems of which the Army does not ordinarily take cognizance because in most Army camps civilian employees do not live on the Post. Had anyone felt impelled to beat his wife or steal a neighbor's spoons there was not much the Army could do but deposit the culprit on a pink promontory of tufa outside the gate, to be picked up, perhaps, by a New Mexico officer of the law out hunting cattle rustlers. Fortunately, we were by and large a pretty law-abiding bunch, more given to argument and mildly eccentric behavior than to overt breaches of the peace. Nevertheless rumor has it that more than one conscientious game warden stood helplessly outside the domain marked off by frequent signs saying "Peligro—Probiedad del Goberno," suspecting with some justice that the random shots he heard were aimed not at hypothetical battleships, but at quite substantial rabbits.

We were also in a political no-man's land. We could not vote in New Mexico, even after we had established residence and paid our income tax. Most of us, as war migrants, had lost absentee voting privileges, and a number of responsible members of our youthful community had not been old enough or settled enough to vote in previous elections. Of course the Army had authority to cope with anyone who damaged government property or interfered with the speedy execution of the Project, and for affairs inside the Tech Area there was a governing board and a council made up of members of the technical hierarchy which controlled civilian activities directly connected with the bomb. Yet as the community of wives and children grew and as diverse patterns of living emerged, there turned out to be a multitude of details that seemed to be nobody's business. The novelty of life at Los Alamos made every man his own politician. Abuses that we had taken for granted and rights that we had never bothered to exercise in conventional communities suddenly seemed important. Then too we were gripped by the panic that so easily besets a civilian confronted by the stern exigencies of military discipline. The fence was literally, as well as figuratively, completing its encirclement, and those convenient holes in it, through which small boys and evening strollers had entered nearby canyons, were being plugged up. The innate American preference for being governed by almost any guy in tweeds or a sack suit rather than by an efficient chap in uniform soon led to agitation for a civilian representative body.

A first, appointed council was short-lived. It was not a standard feature of an Army Post and seemed to compromise military authority. However, civilian employees, who had been promised some such loophole in military control when they joined the Laboratory, were not willing to let the idea die, and when a new commanding officer arrived with instructions to secure greater civilian cooperation, the way was clear for a fresh start. A Town Council of six members, drawn from Tech Area and Post personnel, was elected and began to function in June 1943.

Perhaps, as skeptics pointed out, the Town Council didn't govern. It never made of Los Alamos a paradise of convenience and gracious living, but as a place for letting off steam it was a great success. As one Council succeeded another at six-month intervals, meetings became longer, attendance of nonmembers larger, and the topics discussed more diverse and controversial. Members of the first two Councils could generally count on spending Monday evenings in the quiet seclusion of the private dining room at Fuller Lodge and being home by nine-thirty. As time went on, a growing audience of interested citizens joined those who came to register a specific protest. Frequently meetings were moved to the larger main dining room and arguments had to be cut short at eleven. The machinists through their organization, the Tech Area Social Club, began sending a regular observer; so did the Mesa Club, the women's organization for the propagation of culture and the arts. The Laboratory Director soon found that it saved a lot of correspondence if one of his assistants could answer questions on the spot; and the director of the Housing Office, which dealt with maids and laundries as well as houses, found that most complaints eventually landed on her doorstep so she came regularly. A representative from Post Command became an important figure in Council transactions, explaining why some innocent request could not be granted and, on occasion, convincing his superiors that those confounded civilians had a good case. His presence, however helpful, made clear what we already knew, that the Council could never be a true policy-making body, but it could and did insist on being informed of regulations affecting the community before they went into effect. So long as the military authorities remembered to do this, major eruptions were usually avoided.

Bylaws and election rules were always changing. As reliance on the Council as intermediary increased, it tried to make itself more fully representative. When the first one was elected the population was numbered in hundreds, and to all intents and purposes everybody knew each other. The list of nominees was made up from petitions with thirty-five signatures prepared by friends of likely-looking councilmen. The first three Councils were made up entirely of residents of the original green houses and, with a couple of exceptions, of Tech Area employees or their wives. The fourth Council had one member from Morganville, but by this time McKeeville had sprung out of the mud nearby, there was a rapidly growing hutment and trailer area, and dormitories housed several hundred machinists.

The mushroomlike growth was a constant source of jokes. One might be picking tall white yuccas and fiery paintbrush in a quiet mountain meadow one Sunday and come back two weeks later to find it covered with government trailers or Nissen huts. But for the people who lived in the new areas the joke was not funny. We in the green houses found our surroundings something short of luxurious, with ceilings far from soundproof and furnace men treating us like some rare orchid that had to be kept at 90 degrees. But when we learned that people in the trailers sometimes waited weeks to get their plumbing connected and had to take showers in unheated latrines, we realized that they needed a good old ward heeler to plead their case. The machinists in their dormitories, many of them old union men, readily organized a pressure group, but the trailer and hutment residents, who worked variously for the Tech Area, Post, and miscellaneous contractors, did not get together so easily. So the fourth Town Council tried to ensure a wider representation in its successor by increasing the membership from six to eight and launching a campaign to get the newer sections of the community to nominate candidates. We were less successful in this than we hoped, but the machinists' candidate, who lived in the trailer area, was elected, and the people there, even though not represented in proportion to their numbers, began to bring their problems to the Council, which thereafter devoted much attention to them.

Many busy people took time to serve on Town Council. Viki Weiss-kopf, of Viennese upbringing and German training, was a member of two Councils and chairman of one. As a group leader in theoretical physics he might have pleaded that he could not spend several hours a week on problems of maid service and milk delivery, but he was one of the most active troubleshooters. Sam Allison, an associate director of the Laboratory, served for six months, as did Harry Allen, a key man in the busy procurement section. The Council on which I served, the fourth, was a fairly typical group. Weisskopf, our chairman, and Roger Sutton, representing the dormitories, were serving second terms. Tony Grubman proved particularly good at tracking down reports of trouble and he served on the next Council as chairman. Bob Van Gemert was the voice of McKeeville and Morganville. Jane Kamm, who kept house, worked full time in charge of documents in the Tech Area Library, and served as Council secretary as well, represented working women. I taught in the high school, but my constituency was presumably housewives and mothers, and I had only to list the day's minor trials to make a full contribution to the agenda.

Most meetings were fairly routine. At about a quarter to eight, the Council and the liaison advisers assembled around one of two tables in the private dining room at the Lodge and lit their cigarettes. The audience, mostly women delayed by putting babies to bed and washing dishes, drifted in after the meeting began, sat around the second table as long as the chairs lasted or perched along the raised hearth of the big stone fireplace, and took out their knitting. A few traffic cases were heard; reports, usually inconclusive, were made on questions raised at the previous meeting; new questions were referred to the Post representative or the director of the Housing Office. Matters that lay outside either province were delegated to a Council member for investigation. One problem might be discussed in detail, and after two or three hours we all went home. But perhaps twice in each Council's term, the meeting verged on the sensational; feeling ran high, and between bursts of oratory a star performer would plunge the audience into gales of laughter. There was one memorable meeting when Dick Feynman tried to confound the Army and forestall higher meal prices at Fuller Lodge by recourse to higher mathematics, and an even more dramatic evening devoted to sex life in the dorms when a record audience hung over the balcony in the crowded main dining room, enjoying every word of innuendo and humor at the expense of their dormitory friends. The scandal turned out to be no more significant than the incident that started it. During the first of recurrent housing shortages a young physicist, who did not wish to have an occupant assigned to the second bed in his small room, adopted the simple expedient of laying on it each night a silk and lace creation belonging to his wife, who had not yet arrived. It solved his problem but caused a mild stir. From time to time, the Council received reports of "goings-on" in a women's dormitory, but the visitor was usually identified as a soldier-husband on the Post. One complaint concerned the introduction of "a female" into the men's dorm, but she turned out to be a horse.

Meanwhile the dorms increased in number, and people were assigned to them quickly without regard to congeniality of tastes and habits. After numerous reports of visitors at unseemly hours, disturbing sleep and/or moral sensibilities, the Housing Office and the Post commander posted MPs in all dorms without consulting the residents. A howl of protest arose. Men and women in the older dormitories were for the most part college graduates experienced both in dormitory life and in setting up enough rules to live comfortably together; beyond that point they preferred to mind their own business. They were furious at the appearance of the MPs—a few at the slur on their reputations, the rest at the extension of military supervision. They attended the next Council meeting in force and demanded withdrawal of the MPs. In the course of some rather acid repartee an Army spokesman referred to the increase in the syphilis rate, and the Council member representing the women's dorms burst into tears. The machinists, usually the first to take umbrage, were philosophical about their uninvited guest. "The MP's a nice guy," said one. "If he looks lonesome we give him a beer."

Sex had its ups and downs, but the food problem was always with us. Scarcely a meeting ended without mention of the Commissary and wherein it fell short of Charles or S. S. Pierce. Accustomed to shopping in a small New England village where winter vegetables consisted of carrots, turnips, and cabbage, I was less shocked than the Californians by wilted lettuce or oranges priced at thirty cents a dozen. My boiling point came over the milk shortage when, after teaching all morning, feeding my family, and rushing to the Commissary to catch the last delivery, I found the milk rack empty and had to make a second trip after the next truck arrived and then carry home five or six quarts. Complaints that prices were higher than in Santa Fe and Española sparked a Council-sponsored survey which demonstrated that, even with our 10% service charge, prices on the Hill averaged 10% lower than elsewhere in the area. The Army had subsidized a certain producer by buying feed to encourage him to install new equipment and keep more cows, but in the winter of 1944–45 orders came from Washington to stop all subsidies and up went the price of milk from sixteen to eighteen cents a quart. The Army put it to the civilians by way of the Council that we could not have both a cheap milk supply and a dependable one; the reply was that we were paying two cents above the ceiling price in Santa Fe and that it ill became one arm of government to break the regulations of another. The Army won that round with a ruling by the Office of Price Administration sanctioning this local violation. Meanwhile the Council learned a lot about the price of feed and beef on the hoof and the number of acres of New Mexico—fifty-one—required to feed one cow. The assurance of an adequate milk supply was premature, and we were shortly threatened with rationing. Again the Council argued late into the evening. In the end, the amount one person could take out at one time was restricted, but there was nothing to prevent our coming back later for a second lot, and that was what mothers of hard-drinking families had to do.

The maid service too was always in a state of crisis. Whenever a housewife, or group of them, got sufficiently worked up over the fact that Mrs. A., with one child, had two half-days help a week while Mrs. B., with two children, had only one, the Council could expect a session on maids. When I was on the Council it was a dull week that I did not spend four or five hours being waited on by delegations of women or at special meetings. The protagonists were the tired mothers and the tired working gals. I was both, but I could never decide which made me more tired and was not much help to either side. In the hope of achieving a more equitable system of rationing, Hanni Bretscher, a mathematician trained to deal with more abstruse topics, applied herself to setting up categories. To distinguish between a full-time, a two-thirds-time, or half-time working woman was simple, but was one two-year-old male equal in wear, tear, and washing to two five- and seven-year-old females? Women who taught school had priority, for if they stayed home with a sick child it created more general dislocation than the absence of one laboratory assistant. Throw in all the pregnant women with or without children, with or without jobs, and the women fresh home from the hospital with new infants (first, second, or third) and you get a preliminary idea of what an achievement it was when Hanni produced a system that appreciably reduced the number of women who left the maids' office in hysterics. Finally the Army found more buses to bring women from the pueblos and villages in the valley and even further afield, and Peggy Thompson of the Housing Office drew up a kind of Fair Employment Practices Act that did much to prevent sniping and to make the work more attractive.

HOUSEHOLD HELP

We recognize that under present conditions, having household help at all involves a great many problems, and necessitates the full cooperation of all people concerned. In most other parts of the country there is no help to be had. Since the employment of the household help is a three way endeavor, we wish to offer the following suggestions which we hope will help to clarify the relationship between the employers and the employees, as well as their mutual obligations, and to simplify the work of the housing office.

We suggest that a set of standards touching on the following subjects be drawn up by the Housing Office, and be given to every present and future employer: hiring, hours, wages, substitutes, priority, and transportation of the employees to and from the site.

We suggest that the employees be told of these standards.

> Jean Bacher
> Alice Cornog
> Mary Mack
> Kitty Oppenheimer
> Charlotte Serber
> Alice Smith
> Etta Woodward.

1. HIRING
   A. All hiring or changing should be done through the housing office.
   B. No permanent change should be made by the Housing Office unless the employer is notified.
   C. An employee may request a change in employer if she is not happy working for said employer.
   D. In case of "C," the change would not be made until a suitable substitute is found.

2. HOURS
   8:15 to 12:00 and 1:00 to 4:45
   Employers should realize that the busses are on time if possible, but the weather may play a large part in the promptness of the girls. Those people who live a long way from the bus

Rules for household help. (Original provided by Jean Bacher) stop will necessarily be deprived of a few minutes in the late afternoon, and in the early morning, as the busses DO NOT wait for the girls.

One of the reasons for absenteeism in our girls is that all the Pueblos have certain Feast days, and these girls are expected to attend, and we expect them to do so.

3. WAGES
   A. $1.50 per half day. The girls provide their own lunches.
   B. If bad weather or transportation difficulties prevent the girls from arriving on time, they should be paid their full wage.
   C. In cases where a girl is regularly scheduled for a home, and the employer decides at the last minute she does not need the girl, or the door is locked, the employer shall pay the girl for the full half day.
   D. An employer who finds she will not need her regular girl should notify the Housing Office at least one half day in advance.
   E. An employer only needing half a morning, or afternoon, should notify the Housing Office of the fact, and not pay the girl only 75¢ and send her back.

4. SUBSTITUTE ARRANGEMENTS
   A. There should be continued, the present arrangement of paying 25¢ a month per family to take care of payment of unused substitutes.
   B. An employee should notify the Housing Office and the employer when she knows she will not be coming.
   C. In the event of illness or emergency a girl may be "Borrowed" for a short period as it is recognized that illness has first priority. The girl will be returned to her regular schedule as soon as the emergency passes.
   D. In order that the girls do the work required of them as efficiently as possible, it is suggested that a very complete list be left. This is most important when a girl is new, or is a substitute. It has been found that while the girls are very willing, they do not always know what the employer wants done.
   E. The Housing Office would like a list of women who could use extra help when there are too many substitutes. A list of things to be done in the event that the Housing Office

could send an extra girl unannounced would facilitate matters.

F. From time to time there are dire shortages of help. Therefore the Housing Office would like a list of women who could spare their regular help without too much inconvenience. In such cases an extra girl would be sent to those employers as soon as one became available.

G. In the event that a regular girl does not come, and the employer does not want a substitute, the Housing Office should be told. The Housing Office will send substitutes if it is at all possible.

5. PRIORITIES

A. Priority in allotting employees should be granted, with preference within each group, depending on the circumstances:
    1. Illness, or pregnancy, children
    2. Working wives, children
    3. Working wives without children
    4. Non-working wives (when there is illness in this group the priority is, naturally, raised to 1)

    Note: We realize that cases will arise in which priorities should be modified, at the discretion of the Housing Office, because of the nature of an employer's occupation, of the number of people affected; e.g. in the case of a school teacher, whose absence would affect a great many people.

6. TRANSPORTATION

The Post administration is doing all in its power to provide safe and adequate transportation for the Household Help. There are times when the busses are late, or have mechanical difficulties, and these are unavoidable. It is to be understood that the transportation is a very difficult part of the whole business of having the girls here, and it is to be hoped that all the employers will cooperate in seeing that the girls are on time for their busses.

If the employers do not live up these conditions, and if the employees fail to fulfill their part of the conditions their schedules will be discontinued.

Other crises led to meetings intense and explosive: for instance, the case of "the fourteen families" who on arrival had been given three-bedroom apartments when they needed only two and were later threatened with removal to smaller quarters. Rather unimportant these matters seem in retrospect and petty indeed they must appear to people who think of Los Alamos in terms of nuclear fission and bombs. Perhaps it was partly the tension to which we could not give vent directly that made us throw ourselves so vehemently into battles over milk delivery, maid service, and whether the Commissary carried bottled artichoke hearts.

Thinking back over Town Council meetings brings a queer assortment of topics to mind—snapping dogs, inadequate restaurant facilities, requests for shoe repair service on the Hill, changes in movie schedules, overcrowding in the public laundries. The Post Exchanges were frequently under fire in regard to hours, prices, and the quality of food served there. I remember an impassioned speech by a machinist on the inadequacy of the bus service to Santa Fe. He pointed out that it was causing the Project to lose working time and cited the sad case of a fellow machinist who, after one or two drinks in a Santa Fe bar, could find no bus to Los Alamos so had a few more and did not get back to work for two days.

In mid-1944, with a national election in the offing, people became agitated about impending disenfranchisement. There had once been a ballot box at Los Alamos, but it disappeared with the Ranch School. Rumor said that the sheriff of Sandoval County, a Republican worried about his job in a Democratic state, did not care to trust his political future to the votes of outsiders on the Hill. It was explained to him that none of us was interestd in county politics, and for a time the prospect of being able to vote looked bright, but when a few volunteers made the seventy-five-mile trip to the county seat at Bernalillo to register they were put off with various excuses, and no one at Los Alamos was allowed to do so.

The rifle range was a chronic problem which owed its solution rather to the hand of fate than to the sage deliberations of the Council. A rifle range, unlike a town council, is an institution which an Army Post is expected to support. It was a fine range, carefully laid out in the days when the mesa seemed large, the Project small, and the need for town planning infinitely remote. The trouble was that it occupied the highest point of open ground anywhere about. There was nothing to prevent bullets from spraying over the surrounding terrain in which were located the golf course, horse corrals, baseball field, and popular picnic places and where riding and hiking trails started up the mountains. Small boys loved the place. After every spell of shooting they descended like vultures, and the lead soldier business flourished. But to their chicken-hearted elders the situation seemed perilous in the extreme, and it was with no small pleasure that the Council entertained petitions requesting that use of the range be discontinued. Eleanor Jette, an avid horsewoman who had more than once taken shelter in the lee of a canyon wall or retreated back up the mountain to avoid whizzing bullets, was appointed an admittedly unobjective member of a committee of two to investigate. The Army liaison officer was the other. Early one afternoon they met to survey the range and recommend safety measures, but as they approached the area they were met with smoke and the shriek of sirens. The range was blazing merrily, and the part that was visible outside the blaze was a joyous wreck. Eleanor looked at the officer, and he looked at Eleanor. "A neat solution to a burning question," said she.

Setting up a community from scratch is rather like stocking pantry shelves after moving: you get in the turtle soup and anchovy paste and find you have forgotten the salt and Dutch Cleanser. The Army was well equipped to deal with spies and saboteurs but had apparently neglected that most common of modern malefactions, the improper operation and disposal of a motor vehicle. It could ground its own drivers but had no mechanism for dealing with a civilian. At times it seemed as if every erstwhile driver of a light delivery truck had found his way to Site Y and was careening around the mesa in a jeep or Army car. But they were not the only offenders, for it was well known that in Europe no self-respecting theoretical physicist drove a car at all and that in America he did not drive well. Some were learning at Los Alamos.

One of the Council's first efforts was to set up a system for coping with traffic violations. Army and Council together made the rules, MPs presented the tickets, and the culprits were supposed to appear before the Council's next meeting for a hearing. A fine of $3.00 was set for the first violation, $5.00 for the second, and $10.00 for the third. Beyond that the Council in its innocence did not care to look. Neither Army nor Council was authorized to collect and disburse funds so fines were turned over to the Red Cross. This voluntary system generally worked.

Only one young man of principle (what principle was not clear) refused to pay until argued into cooperation by the Laboratory Director himself.

The traffic violation business boomed and then without any notable improvement in driving techniques faltered and died. It seemed that the Army had trouble enough with civilians without arresting them. The Council found the lull suspicious; negotiations followed, and a new regime was established. Post command promised more men to patrol the roads; an officer collected uncontested fines, and those who did not think they had had a fair deal appeared before the Council, carrying ticket in one hand and leading arresting MP by the other. Meanwhile parking space dwindled as public buildings sprouted additions and the population grew. The Fire Department worried about obstruction of roads, and "no parking" signs appeared in spots long considered sacred by householders and shopping mothers. We amateur magistrates on the Council readily accepted excuses—a car had stalled in a snowstorm, a woman had parked illegally while extracting a sick friend from the PX, a parking sign had blown down—and enjoyed being tough only when a belligerent offender tried to tell us how these things were handled in Kalamazoo or Brooklyn. The horrid prospect of trying to conform to traffic regulations in all forty-eight states and several hundred home towns sharpened our enthusiasm for the benevolent activities of the Red Cross.

It was agitation in the Council that finally led to the laying of a sidewalk along the well-traveled West Road and to the setting up of small play yards with swings and sandboxes throughout the residential areas. Another achievement, though a temporary one, was rent adjustment. Rents varied according to the salary of the chief wage earner in the family, but the rate was based on brackets, not on a sliding scale, so that a small raise might put a worker in a higher bracket and hence decrease the net income. Rents of support personnel were based on hourly pay for a forty-hour week, whereas salaried employees worked forty-eight hours, plus many hours of unpaid overtime. It took months and a lot of correspondence to convince a high enough authority of the inequity of this arrangement and to obtain an adjustment, and then the retroactive clause of one month seemed inadequate to people who had been paying at too high a rate for two years. The argument started all over again when the whole project went on a forty-hour week at the end of the war.

After the war there also occurred the most serious of a succession of utilities crises. To conserve the electricity supply, which had often been erratic, power was scheduled to go off when necessary during alternate half-hours from 5 P.M. on, and often it did. No sooner had the power supply increased than a water shortage became acute. The idea gained currency that we should not pay twelve dollars a month for utilities which we had enjoyed so sparingly. Again Town Council made a good storm center, and in so doing nearly brought about its own demise.* The Council elected in October 1945 had a particularly harrowing term. Both Laboratory and individual planning were in flux. Many people were leaving; voting showed a not unexpected apathy; and the new Council could not always muster a quorum. Its minutes reflected the bitterness of residents over the water shortage and their frustration at failure to obtain a guarantee of future supplies. A motion that the Council resign in protest was defeated by one vote. As a compromise the members shortened their terms and advanced the election of successors. They departed on a plaintive note: "The exhausted Council has appointed Mr. Taschek to serve with the new Council for a period of one month."

The Council hoped that a new election would prove that civilians at Los Alamos were behind it. Indeed, the voting showed a renaissance of interest, which may be a sign that the community and its citizens have come of age politically. There were nineteen candidates for eight places. The new town newspaper ran a voters' guide. One group tagged itself ALAT, the Action in Los Alamos Ticket, and elected its entire slate. A ballot box was placed in the Commissary, a device that helped to produce over a thousand ballots compared with previous highs of three to four hundred. Perhaps there is something about an Army Commissary, however well managed, that stimulates the urge to direct political action.

A great deal has been implied about the gulf between civilians and military, but the officers who brought their families to Los Alamos were good friends and neighbors. If socially some line seemed to exist it was no more strongly defined than that which in a university community makes the doctors, the scientists, or the economists tend to fraternize with their professional colleagues. But there was a line be-

---

*For Council history after late December 1945, I rely on information sent to me in Chicago by Eleanor Jette, supplemented by later refugees from Los Alamos, most of whom were too occupied by the red tape of departure to be involved in politics.

tween those in uniform and those who were not. It was the line that separates those who are free to question, to debate, and to accept majority decisions and those who, staunch democrats though they may be, have to take orders. That the atomic bomb might not yet have been completed without the framework provided by the military we are well aware, but the civilians who have left Los Alamos are sure that they prefer to live permanently under that clumsier system represented by the spontaneous, if at times unproductive, leadership of the Town Council.

Shirley B. Barnett

Shirley Barnett was an Army wife at Los Alamos, the only one represented in this book. Captain Henry Barnett, her husband, was the popular pediatrician at Los Alamos and was, at one time, head of the hospital. Mrs. Barnett was secretary to the Personnel Director and, later, a secretary to Dr. Oppenheimer.

The Barnetts moved to New York in 1946. Henry taught at Cornell Medical College, then became Founding Chairman and Professor of Pediatrics at the Albert Einstein College of Medicine. He is a Senior Member of the Institute of Medicine of the National Academy of Science and now serves as Medical Director of the Children's Aid Society in New York City. During these 41 years they reared two children and traveled extensively (part work, part play). Shirley has held a variety of salaried jobs—as secretary at McGraw-Hill, assistant for an art conservator, and a staff member working in the development office of an elite boys' school. She now works as a mediator between children and parents referred to a PINS program (persons in need of supervision) by the Family Court.

7

OPERATION LOS ALAMOS

Shirley B. Barnett

Our hospital had a "view of the lake." Perhaps that's putting it a little strongly, since the lake was rather more in the dimension of a pond, or puddle. It was practically overgrown with weeds in summer and only reached decent proportions during the spring thaw. However, it was a body of water (one of the few in that section of New Mexico) and the hospital faced it on one side. On the other side of the pond was the Tech Area.

My first view of the hospital found me completely unprepared. Being a city girl, born and bred, and having become accustomed to the large, impressive ways of modern city hospitals, I thought this small, one-story building with its air of a community meeting-house looked very little like a hospital. We drove up to Los Alamos in the glory of a July afternoon in 1943 and were met by the hospital staff—one doctor (Jim Nolan, obstetrician, gynecologist, surgeon, 1st Lt., AUS) and three nurses. The rest of the staff consisted of a medical secretary and two small Indian boys acting as hospital orderlies, messenger boys, and general local color. The hospital had six beds, an operating room, and a few small rooms for offices, pharmacy, and conferences. There was also a large room for a pediatric nursery. At that time it was still thought that the population of Los Alamos would not increase to much over five hundred families and the hospital facilities seemed adequate. Supplies and equipment had been ordered or were already available, and the hospital had been functioning for roughly three months. Certain minor adjustments had to be made in the physical setup. For some bizarre reason, the hospital had been built so that the entrance to the operating room was right off the waiting room. When the operating room was in use, it was necessary to close off the waiting room, and patients, or prospective patients, had to wait outdoors or wherever else seemed handy. This situation was quickly corrected, but the re-routing of patients from the old entrance to the new was a major undertaking.

When we arrived, there had been no serious illnesses, but only the multitude of small ailments that occur when groups of people from various parts of the country are brought together. "Itis," the plague of Los Alamos, had begun. Its full name was "Santa Fe-itis," and it was the same intestinal flu that had been spreading throughout the country under various names in 1943. We were never completely without it in all of our stay at the Project. Newcomers were always warned by oldtimers of the possibility of being stricken, and the oldtimers were one hundred percent right!

My husband, Henry, the area pediatrician (sometimes referred to as the "miniature doctor" by his medical confreres) was kept going at a good clip from the beginning. In addition to appointments during the day, he had a fair number of house calls to make each evening. They proved to be something of a problem at first. Los Alamos housing was arranged so haphazardly that the way to a patient's house was filled with booby traps. The house numbers followed no order, nor was there any accurate way of giving descriptions of locations since all houses looked alike and there were no streets—let alone street names. This led to a lot of unnecessary door-knocking until the doctors got thoroughly familiar with the strange layout.

Our communications system was a little difficult, too. Telephones had been installed in the homes of only the few people who might be needed in emergencies or who had to be reached at odd hours. The doctors qualified, but it was necessary for anyone trying to reach a doctor, plumber, electrician, etc., after regular hours either to locate a telephone in his own neighborhood or to hot-foot it to their homes. The doctors' telephone was a party line with three extensions: No. 1 for Jim, No. 2 for my husband, and No. 3 for Louis Hempelmann, the radiologist employed in the Tech Area. Our rings were 1, 2, and 3 in the same order. Several interesting events can be laid directly to our party line. Since the work was heavy in all branches of medicine, Jim and Henry took calls for each other from time to time. Louis helped them both out in the evenings. During the first few months when the telephone rang at night, the chances were that the three doctors would lift their phones simultaneously (who can count rings at 3 A.M.?) and there would begin a chorus of weary and sleepy hellos, which would completely drown out the voice of the person calling. This sometimes went on for a minute or so and then one, two, or very occasionally all three of the doctors would hang up, figuring that this was someone else's call. By this time, however, they were sufficiently awake so that when the patient called back, the doctor for whom the bell tolled would answer. After a while, the doctors grew cagey about these calls. Although they would all lift their phones (if it was late at night), no one would say anything, breathing heavily ("I know you're there"), waiting for someone else to begin. The doctor who gave the first mumbled greeting would have to make the house call. Someone eventually would weaken, and the other two could hang up with sighs of satisfaction. The doctors remedied this situation with a system of "nights on call."

When a telephone call to a doctor did not seem feasible, we could expect a personal visit. My husband and I are both sound sleepers and often did not hear a knock at our door. On these occasions, we would be awakened by the noise of someone stumbling around in our living room, cursing softly. The first time this happened I was frightened enough to want to pretend that it was all a bad dream and there positively was no one in our living room. However, I was forced to accept reality when a male voice at our bedroom door inquired if this was Dr. Barnett's residence. To be awakened in this fashion from a sound sleep struck me as informal, to say the least, but we soon got used to it. The one thing we had to remember before going to bed was to close the top of the piano in our living room. One nocturnal visitor, tripping around in the dark, had inadvertently come down rather heavily on the keyboard of the piano, throwing himself and us into a state of wild confusion.

One of the most exciting features of our hospital was the fact that the lights in the operating room could be seen at night for quite a distance. Since the hospital was centrally located, no operation or emergency went unnoticed by the local gentry. I remember waiting one night outside the hospital with Anne, Jim's wife, while Jim and Henry were in the operating room taking care of an emergency. Anne was expecting a baby within a week or two. It was to be the first baby born at Los Alamos and as such was the cause of much comment. When a car drove up and the occupants spotted us standing in the shadows, they asked why the operating room lights were on. When we said we didn't know, they wondered audibly if Anne's baby was being born. Anne stepped out from the shadows and reassured them. As the car drove off, Anne made a fervent wish that her baby be born during the day, so as to assure her some chance of a head start on knowing whether her baby was a boy or a girl. Her wish was not granted, but her child was born during a night of comparative quiet on the mesa. The announcement was made next morning to a proud community, who felt that the birth of its first child was something in the way of a major event and a matter for loud huzzahs.

Our birth rate after this (Anne's baby was born in August 1943) was fairly high. Eighty babies were born during the first year, and about ten a month thereafter. "Rural Free Delivery," people said, jokingly. Henry's pediatric practice increased steadily. The great majority of the babies were first children, since this was a community composed largely of young couples. A nursery school was one of the first community

Eighty babies were born during the first year, and about ten a month thereafter. . . . The great majority of babies were first children, since this was a community composed largely of young couples. (Los Alamos National Laboratory)

A nursery school was one of the first community projects set up, and one of [the doctor's] pleasantest duties was his daily visit to the school for physical checkups. (Los Alamos National Laboratory)

projects set up, and one of Henry's pleasantest duties was his daily visit to the school for physical checkups.

In spite of the comparatively small area covered by the living quarters at Los Alamos, the doctors traveled enough to make a car necessary. A car was assigned to each doctor, and Henry became the proud possessor of a jeep—one of the very few in use on the Project at that time. His pediatric patients loved the jeep dearly and were willing to have the doctor come at any time in hope of getting a ride in it. The jeep was finally exchanged for a coupe, but for the small-fry the association stuck: where a jeep was, Dr. Barnett was.

The hospital, like most Army installations at Los Alamos, was a service offered to the scientists and their families to ensure a minimum amount of time out because of illness. The doctors were aware of this and eager to do anything they could in the way of preventive and immediate care, since they appreciated the importance of speed in the work being done. They were very much assisted in this by the willingness and cooperation shown by the community and because they were able to see all patients when symptoms first appeared. It is true that there was no choice of patient or doctor, and this sometimes made difficulties. But the desire on the part of the doctors to keep the quality of the medical care for the greatest good was always uppermost. There were clashes between patients and doctors, and now and then some bad feeling. On the whole, however, there was too much interdependence to make it possible for anyone to indulge in sulks, and gradually trust and understanding grew, but not without incidents.

Before coming to Los Alamos, neither Jim nor Henry had been in private practice. Henry had been on the full-time faculty of a medical school, and Jim on the full-time staff of a hospital. They both had had a great deal of hospital practice, but one of their difficulties here was deciding how many of their troubles were common to all private practices and how many were specific to Los Alamos. As their practices grew, they became more able to relate the problems to their proper causes. At first Henry was stumped by a patient who informed him that she knew there were two kinds of colds, a Vicks VapoRub cold and a tincture of benzoine cold, and asked that the cold her child had at the moment be properly identified. But after a while these were no longer problems to Henry or Jim. They could identify a Vicks or a tincture of benzoine cold at a distance of fifteen miles on a clear day.

All of the senior doctors at the hospital were specialists in their fields, and with one exception, all had passed their specialty board examinations. Their credentials came to be accepted by the community, but not before Jim and Henry, setting an example, had plastered their office walls with every bit of written evidence they owned showing that they had graduated from medical school, received a license to practice medicine, received a certificate from a specialty board, and were generally known to be fit and able. The decision to post all of their diplomas came after a soul-searching conference at which they decided that their public relations were bad and that what they needed was a little more ballyhoo.

Jim, in his capacity as surgeon, used the facilities of Bruns General Hospital in Santa Fe for cases requiring equipment or specific treatment which our hospital was unable to supply. After the first year, when our hospital was enlarged both in staff and physical layout, this was no longer necessary. However, in the beginning, it sometimes became a matter of dispute between Jim and his amateur doctor advisers as to where a patient should be treated—at Los Alamos or at Bruns. Jim finally found a perfect pattern for avoiding acrimonious discussion on medical subjects with a "doctor's helper" during a visit from the supervisor of a man who had broken his leg. The supervisor wanted to know what was being done. After Jim explained the procedure being followed, the conversation as I heard it went something like this:

Amateur-Doctor Adviser: "I'm very worried about this man—need him on the job, and I wonder if he couldn't be better taken care of at Bruns."

Jim: "No. Whatever can be done for him is being done here. Nothing can be done at Bruns to speed up the healing beyond what we're doing."

A-D. A.: "Well, I don't know. I think perhaps he might be better off at Bruns. We'd get him back on the job sooner. My advice would be to send him down there."

Jim, at this point, was obviously thrashing around in his mind for some way to stop this.

Jim: "Tell me, how is the work going in your department?"

A-D. A.: "Fine. But about this. . . ."

Jim: "I mean, are you getting the work done? You know I'm very interested in this because I think it's important to the whole Project. Do you need any help in your department? Perhaps I could come in for a few minutes and set a few things right. You know, I've often thought that a new and uninformed point of view could do wonders in these scientific things."

A-D. A.: "Well, I hardly think. . . ."

Jim: "Oh, that's all right. But if you need advice on anything, just call me. Be glad to help."

A-D. A.:"Well, I—well, I—thanks a lot, Doctor. I'll be around later in the week."

The analogy was forcefully drawn, and Jim had found a formula which solved this problem.

The natural hazards of transplanting a large group of urban dwellers into a country where vigorous outdoor exercise is very much the thing took its toll. There were horseback-riding accidents, skiing accidents, and even one Ping-Pong accident. Touch football provided its share of dislocations and sprains, with tennis trailing along behind. By the time the community had reached its top population (around 7000), our vital statistics in relation to accidents were on a par with any.

There were, I'm sure, aspects of medicine as it was practiced at Los Alamos which bore no relation to medicine practiced anywhere else. There was, for instance, the matter of rescue parties. Twice during the winter of 1943–44, a doctor had to set out with a rescue party to help a too-ambitious athlete. The first rescue came as a result of a telephone call from a ranger station on Truchas Peak. A party had set out early one Sunday to climb Truchas, the highest peak in the vicinity. Late in the afternoon, a counting of noses revealed that one of the party had disappeared. The others immediately organized a search, knowing that it would be dark soon and that the missing boy had neither matches, flashlight, nor food. When their efforts proved fruitless, they walked to a ranger station some miles away to call for help. When the call came in at about 11 P.M., Henry, Jim, and Louis drew lots to see who should go. It was a cold, cold night and Louis (chosen by fate) was bundled up in a combat uniform, given Hershey bars and whiskey, and wished Godspeed. He returned late the following morning to report that after they had searched and called frantically most of the night with no success, the missing boy had calmly walked into the ranger hut at daybreak, cold but unharmed. Realizing he was lost, he had sensibly decided against stumbling around in the dark, had curled up against a rock and slept until daybreak, when he was able to find the trail to the ranger station. This incident was comparatively minor; except for loss of sleep, and the discussion it provoked about setting up regulations for all hiking parties, it hardly caused a ripple.

The second rescue involved a more adventurous group who had left the Hill on a sparkling Saturday morning for an overnight ski trip. It was April, the snow was still deep in the mountains, and the eight young people were all strong skiers. At a little after midnight, however, they called in for help. One of the skiers had broken his leg. To call, two of them had skied thirteen miles to a ranch, while the rest stayed in a shack with the injured man.

The doctors arranged to meet the two young skiers at the ranch and went into a huddle to plan the rescue. They would need an ambulance, a toboggan, and a skiing doctor. They arranged for the ambulance, a driver, and food and medical supplies. Even after rousing people all over the mesa, they failed to find a toboggan. And they discovered that the only skier among them was Henry. Henry was a weak skier at best, and he had been up for two nights with a hospitalized child. Then someone remembered a doctor at Bruns Hospital who not only owned a toboggan but also had trained Army troops in ski rescue techniques. This was obviously the man for the job. Henry breathed a sigh of relief. The Bruns doctor, reached by phone, was glad to lend his toboggan but proved to be in no condition for a ski trip: he had had all his upper teeth extracted that afternoon. Henry, once again the focus of all eyes, took up the phone to receive advice and benedictions from him. The planners, deciding they needed a fourth skier to help manage the toboggan over the thirteen miles between ranch and shack, selected a young man and sent someone to waken him. He was startled at the request but agreed to go.

The rescue party left the Hill at about two, Monday morning, picked up the toboggan in Santa Fe, met the boys at the ranch, and started off for the shack. The toboggan was heavy and the going was slow. It was evening before they reached the injured man. After Henry had splinted the broken leg, given the man morphine, and distributed supplies, they all rested. The next morning, they started down to the ranch, taking turns pulling the toboggan and all pitching in when it had to be carried. The toboggan was heavier now, and the going was slower. New snow began to fall, and the crusted snow on the ground started to give way so that they sometimes were in drifts to their thighs. They broke into a shack for shelter that night and finally reached the ranch and the ambulance at noon on Wednesday.

On the whole, the group—adventurous skiers and rescue party alike—came through in fairly good shape. The man with the broken leg was cared for at Bruns Hospital, and most of the others spent the next eighteen hours sleeping. Henry, however, felt he would not survive another trip like that. From then on, he heartily encouraged the rest of the medical staff to take up skiing and helped form a committee to pass on all plans for hiking, hunting, and skiing trips. No other ski rescues were necessary.

Another job undertaken by the medical staff was inspection of the messes and PXs once a week and general consultant duties on matters affecting water supply, milk, etc. Our reservoir was filled from mountain streams and the water was chlorinated and filtered. In spite of the filters, there was a reported case of a woman who arrived at the hospital one afternoon clutching a jar of water in which reposed a worm, no thicker than a sewing thread, which had arrived at her home via the kitchen tap. She was a little bewildered and more than a little indignant and had to be assured that this was not a common occurrence, nor one which was officially encouraged. She was told of the chow mein which flows from the taps in San Francisco and reminded of the S. J. Perelman story of the Filipino houseboy who arrived via the tap. She left still unpersuaded that this was an uncommon performance on the part of the local worms.

The doctors took over, to a limited extent, the problem of pets. With one exception, all of the doctors were dog or cat owners. Although we had an excellent veterinarian on the Post, the doctors, rather than take advantage of professional courtesy, became their own and each other's veterinarians. When our dog broke his leg, his cast was applied by the hospital surgeon. Henry gave advice on the care and feeding of puppies. An illness, or even loss of appetite in a dog, called for a consultation, and treatments were almost always effective. The problem of the cat who on one occasion climbed up the side of a wall in her owner's apartment seemed insoluble however, since no one knew how to apply psychoanalysis to a cat.

By winter of 1944 it became evident that another doctor was needed at the hospital. Since the three doctors then at Los Alamos were all from St. Louis (had, in fact, all graduated in the same class at medical school), St. Louis was again chosen as the hunting ground, and Paul Hagemann, a practicing internist, was unanimously chosen. Paul expressed interest. A civilian at that time, he applied for his Army commission after a visit to Los Alamos and arrived with his family in April of 1944. Other changes had been made in the staff by this time. There were more nurses, a pharmacist, laboratory technicians, enlisted men to act as hospital orderlies, a maintenance staff and considerably more room. Additions to the hospital had been built so that it rambled in a series of T-shaped buildings connected by a central corridor. Soon after Paul's arrival, with the community growing steadily, a general surgeon and an ear, nose, and throat specialist were added to the staff, along with an x-ray technician and still more nurses. By fall of 1944, the hospital staff had grown from eight people to approximately one hundred.

The hospital invested in an intercommunication system (instead of the traditional loud-speakers). At first, the new gadgets were a source of delight to the entire staff. All sorts of highly unimportant pieces of information were transmitted from office to office by the fascinated doctors. Conversations during the first days had a "roger wilco over" tenor with a dash of Dr. Kildare. But the system lacked volume. In order to be heard one had to raise his voice to something approaching a bellow, thereby eliminating the necessity for the intercom. This trouble was eventually eliminated by electronics experts from the Tech Area, but not before almost all the doctors were reduced to mere whispers because of overworked vocal cords. All in all, the hospital had acquired quite an air.

The dental clinic, which had originally consisted of a room tacked on to one end of the hospital, had grown too. First one full-time dentist and a technician, then two full-time dentists and two technicians, and finally a third dentist arrived. I am a little vague about the workings of the dental clinic since my visits there were brief and tinged with the slight touch of hysteria that always attends these trips for me. I remember a large and sunny room. (The fact that the sun is almost always shining when I visit a dentist has always struck me as incongruous since lightning and thunder rumbling in the distance would be much more appropriate to my mood.) Beyond that I dare not go—fantasy always takes over.

In the process of growth the hospital had lost none of its informal charm. It was very easy to see who had had a baby each day by observing which husbands were standing on packing boxes outside the maternity ward windows. Visitor's hours were almost unnecessary at the hospital because of the abundance of packing boxes and the fact that all windows faced outside.

In addition to its regular staff, the hospital boasted of a member whose fidelity to his post was impeccable. His name was Timoshenko. He was an incredibly large, white dog, a cross between a Great Dane and a Russian wolfhound. No description of his physical characteristics could do him justice, but—as a point of information—when he stood on his hind feet he towered over most humans.

Timoshenko had been given to one of the nurses as a joke. He had been adopted by the staff when it was discovered that he put in a minimum of ten hours a day living at the steps of the hospital. He became intimately acquainted with all the hospital routines from the outside looking in. When Timoshenko had achieved his full growth, it was felt that a dog his size would probably be a boon to the K-9 Corps so he was shipped off for training as an attack dog. He was returned about six months later preceded by a courteous but firm letter from the K-9 Corps advising us that although his size and strength were unquestionable, he was clearly a pacifist. No amount of training, they declared, could convert him into a belligerent. He just hated war. However, a change was noted. The K-9 Corps notwithstanding, Ti-

Visitor's hours were almost unnecessary at the hospital because of the abundance of packing boxes and the fact that all windows faced outside. (Los Alamos Historical Museum)

moshenko had learned some things. He could, for instance, knock over any dog in the community and then stand guard over him. He did this in the best-natured manner imaginable—more like a dog showing off his parlor tricks than in the manner of a combatant. He loved this trick dearly, and people going into the hospital often had to step over not only Timoshenko but also his prostrate victim of the moment. He was discouraged only when he began to practice this trick by the edge of the pond. The dog he was guarding would be completely immersed in the water, and since the principle of oxygen for life was unknown to Timoshenko, we had one or two near drownings.

The hospital's even tenor was not disturbed until a little before the Alamogordo test shot in July 1945. Jim left the hospital at that time to work in the Tech Area on health and safety problems. He was replaced, and this was the beginning of many changes. About a week before the test shot, five of the seven doctors then at the hospital were sent down to Alamogordo to receive instructions on monitoring and to be on hand in case they were needed. They were replaced during this period by a group of doctors from Oak Ridge. Our doctors returned, full of the awe the test shot engendered, and again took up their duties at the hospital. But on August 12, Henry, Paul, and Jim left for Japan with the medical mission to investigate the effects of the atomic bomb on Hiroshima and Nagasaki. Henry and Paul were again replaced by Oak Ridge doctors. When they returned in October, it was for us at least our last few weeks in Los Alamos. We left at the beginning of November.

The two most distinctive aspects of the medicine practiced at Los Alamos were, I believe, the system of medical care and the isolation of the community made necessary by security regulations. Medicine was practiced there on what amounted to a prepaid medical care plan. Opinions of the Los Alamos doctors before they reached our community diverged widely as to the general feasibility of such plans, but whether pro or con, it was quite evident that each doctor did his job honestly and efficiently. At the beginning some in the community may have felt constraint about calling on the doctors as often as they wanted to, but any uncertainty quickly vanished; those who at first took advantage of the medical-care bonanza very soon became accustomed to the idea and stopped making unnecessary demands on the medical staff. The doctors worked hard and the community appreciated it; time set the only limitation on how much or how little they could be asked to do. They voluntarily undertook extracurricular work, such as the classes Henry gave to expectant mothers of first children. They sat in on meetings of all kinds and were an active and important part of community life.

The isolation of the community, coupled with the long hours and high tensions under which people worked, produced some problems of a psychiatric nature. They were fewer, however, than would be imagined under the circumstances. At one time it was suggested that a psychiatrist be added to the hospital staff. The head of the psychiatric service at Oak Ridge came to Los Alamos to determine the need and to arrange for periodic visits. Each doctor had some patients who needed psychotherapy as well as physical care. Each did his best with minor problems and turned over the more serious ones to the visiting psychiatrist. The so-called mad scientist turned out to be a well-balanced person, even when subjected to the tremendous problems and responsibilities involved in the making of the atomic bomb. On the whole, problems of this nature occurred as frequently as in other communities, and some remarkable adjustments were made to the definitely "out of this world" living conditions.

The hospital was but one facet of a unique community. It grew and changed along with the rest of the community, but through it all managed to maintain an air of permanence. I believe that the medical care afforded by the hospital staff was good—or better than good—and that between the community and the hospital there grew an understanding of community medicine and standards of care that proved a source of deep satisfaction to everyone.

JEAN BACHER

Jean Bacher participated in all the social and recreational activities of Los Alamos with real enthusiasm and so can very well write about them at first hand. Her husband, Robert Bacher, led the Bomb Physics Division. For his outstanding work he received the Medal of Merit. Mrs. Bacher had two children and worked as a computor in the Theoretical Physics Division. From Los Alamos the Bachers went to Ithaca, New York, where Dr. Bacher was a Professor of Physics at Cornell University.

After one year at Cornell the Bachers went to Washington—Bob as member of the first Atomic Energy Commission. Jean has participated in all available ways that lead toward the peaceful use of atomic energy, wherever they are. Bob went to Caltech as Head of Physics and later Provost. Jean took an MFA degree in Art at Claremont, practiced art therapy for a time, and helped start the Pasadena Mental Health Center. She likes to travel, especially to New Mexico.

8

FRESH AIR AND ALCOHOL

Jean Bacher

Life at Los Alamos was peculiarly uninhibited and completely unrelaxed. Everyone from the youngest child to the indomitable mother of one of the staff engaged in athletic activity. As a matter of fact, the latter lady, a woman in her sixties or seventies, put many of us to shame by her vigor. It was not surprising to ride a horse fifteen miles, and then on the trail ahead to see her black-clad figure striding along wielding a stout umbrella or stick. We worked hard and we played hard. Exercise was one way to relieve the high tensions and strains of the Project.

The stimulating climate rapidly made even the most sedentary of us something of an athlete. The sun beckoned, and home seemed a drab place from which to escape on Sundays. In the beginning, we took over some of the sports of the schoolboys whose place we had usurped and rode their horses and walked on their trails. Gradually, we went farther and farther afield exploring the mountains and canyons about us. One of the greatest delights of the New Mexican climate is the magical quality of the atmosphere; the clarity of the light is a shimmering and tangible thing. The sun draws into the air the fragrance of the long-needled Western pines and a campfire made of piñon logs has a pungent odor never forgotten. As the Project aged, we acquired a fine ski run and tow, a golf course, tennis courts, baseball fields, and a pasture full of privately owned horses. We had a well-developed line of hobbies in mining, fishing, hunting, mountaineering, and relic hunting. When we had water, there was ice-skating with night illumination in the winter and a swimming pool for children in the summer. There

Gradually, we went farther and farther afield exploring the mountains and canyons about us. (Los Alamos Historical Museum)

was as enthusiastic and fancy a group of square dancers at Los Alamos as one could hope to find anywhere. We had an orchestra and singing groups and chamber music ensembles. We knew beautiful picnic spots. We traveled to the various fiestas and thought we were adept at trading in rugs and silver and pottery.

Many of our recreation facilities were not acquired easily; we had to show real finesse to successfully wangle some of our developments. And what we got was not as fancy a layout as it sounds on first hearing. For instance, the nine-hole golf course was laid out in the horse pasture. It was a barren stretch of field rolling up to the Jemez Mountains which rose just west of the site, and since the place had already been taken over by the horses, fancy hazards such as traps and bunkers were superfluous. The "greens" were protected from roving animals by strings of single wire (acquired in some devious manner), and they became a hazard which enraged the horse-owners. A golfer never knew when a horse might gallop into his drive or kick his ball about the field. It was considered a very sporting course, however, even by some of our British members. A guide was essential for the first few ventures.

The nine-hole golf course was laid out in the horse pasture . . . fancy hazards such as traps and bunkers were superfluous. (Jean Bacher)

As the Project matured, more and more private horses were acquired, and their corrals on the edge of the pasture were a motley lot. Private enterprise and personal inspiration, with only a dump pile to fall back on for material, created a shantytown of stables. It was early discovered that the tops of the coal bins in back of the four-family dwellings were good stout slabs for the sides of shelters and stalls, and that one could occasionally make off with odd sections of corrugated iron. The Army rose in rage, however, when one morning some sections of the current lot of prefabs being erected were missing, and a new barn concocted of them had appeared on the pasture edge.

The pleasures of riding in this mesa and mountain and canyon country were infinite. A few horses had been left behind by the Ranch School but these were soon worn out. For a while the Army kept horses which we could ride at stated times, but these were finally moved away and people acquired their own. There were a few trails for short trips or a fast evening canter, and many miles of wild country to explore on weekends. A small group of women were avid riders and in due course of time encountered adventure. There were of course the mountain lion and the snake but the spy crowned all the exploits. One day as they rode to the top of the ridge behind Los Alamos, they saw clearly across from them a man studying the building laid out below with a spyglass. Of course he was an enemy agent: he looked at the women and turned and ran. They pursued, but he eluded them with excursions into terrain too difficult for horses. With the country's fate at stake, they laid out an elaborate trailing program and finally crept up to a point where they again sighted their quarry. To the amazement and horror of all, one of the women drew a revolver. "I always carry this," she said. "My husband insists that I load the first two shots with blanks, but from there on I can do some good." Before the test could be made, the man escaped. G-2 never told us what happened after that.

The poor cow ponies had a hard time getting used to such civilized menaces as bulldozers, busy jeeps, and Army trucks which roared at them, but hardest of all were the big bangs resulting from experiments with explosives. They came at unpredictable times and, no matter how frequently, always shook at least one nervous animal to the teeth. It made for exciting riding, and beginners had their troubles.

The hospital got pretty weary of treating accidents resulting from our athletic activities. A good number came from thrown riders, but by far the most were from skiing. On winter Monday mornings, the corridors of the hospital were lined with broken legs, ankles, and collarbones and sprains of all description waiting for treatment. Sawyer's Hill was the name of the ski run the boys of the Los Alamos Ranch School had created. Volunteers extended this to a long and beautiful run, with a fine, broad, easy slope at the bottom for children and beginners. A group of young GIs put together a makeshift tow which worked half of Sundays, anyway.

Some friendly soul made a present to one of the big shots of a surplus "weasel." This miniature white tank towed skiers from the bottom of the trail run back to the top many times on a Sunday. It finally met its match in a group of weekend skiers en route up Mt. Redondo, the highest mountain in our group. This peak had an alluring and extensive meadow near its summit, but the drifts on the way up proved too much and the weasel bogged down. Finally, it stayed there and the party had a weary walk home.

Someone persuaded the Army that it could spare a hutment, and one was set up at the foot of Sawyer's Hill. Here there was always a gay Sunday group, eating lunches and warming up at the wood stove. Baby-sitters were eternally scarce and on Sundays were almost non-existent, unless one lived on Bathtub Row and could offer a tub as bait.

A group of young GIs put together a makeshift tow which worked half of Sundays, anyway. (Los Alamos Historical Museum)

As a result, whole families appeared on Sawyer's Hill for the day. Babies were trundled along Indian fashion and set down in the snow and sunshine well out of collision's way while their parents skied. One still had to watch sharply. One small boy whizzed down the hill using his skis as a sled and slid neatly between the skis of a beautiful amateur at the foot. Up in the air and down she went.

Ice-skating was always a poor relation among the winter sports. There was a small pool deep in Los Alamos Canyon, which the school had used. The arguments on how to run a rink and the scarcity of water for flooding it did not produce very good conditions, but I spent many happy hours there and the children never minded the bubbly ice. But it was cold! Shielded from the sun, it was at least ten degrees colder there than on top of the mesa, and at night temperatures might be ten to twenty degrees below zero. In spite of this, we finally produced a rough sort of lighting and with a roaring fire could practice fancy steps after the children were in bed. What with shoveled snow

Ice-skating was always a poor relation among the winter sports. There was a small pool deep in Los Alamos Canyon, which the school had used. The arguments on how to run a rink and the scarcity of water for flooding it did not produce very good conditions, but I spent many happy hours there and the children never minded the bubbly ice. (Los Alamos Historical Museum)

and haphazard floodings, a unique effect was achieved at the end of each season: the ice was thicker at the edges so that unless one could work up considerable centrifugal force one coasted or slid into the center of the rink. A hot toddy usually solved the whole problem.

The outdoor hazards one anticipated meeting before going to Los Alamos never appeared. I never found a rattler in a boot or in a sleeping bag. In fact I never saw one although I clambered around many places where there should have been hundreds. The only snakebite complaint on record came from a laborer engaged in erecting an extension to the hospital. He drifted into the reception room and explained in the half-English, half-Spanish jargon common to all New Mexico natives that a rattlesnake had bitten him. The clerks laughed at him. "A new one, an original stall act," they thought. He left indignantly and to their consternation returned a few moments later with the snake. Rattlers were rare at our altitude. Indian ruins were about the only places one could count on finding them.

How many future archeologists are going to be confounded when they start excavating Los Alamos! The ruins of an ancient tribe already existed there. And now around every back doorstep is a mound of pottery pieces gathered from every old pueblo site up and down the Rio Grande. Mingled with these are samples of all the minerals existing in New Mexico, thrown out to make room for choicer pieces. Malachite, copper, microlite, calcite, lepidolite, silver, fluorite, mica, and turquoise fill the ditches. Only the tiny grains of gold are not there; they are cherished in the bottom of small test tubes.

The Indian ruins in the locale were fascinating, especially to the newcomers who looked on the ancient cave dwellings and compared them, sometimes favorably, with their present living quarters. Frijoles Canyon offered the easiest and best restored series of ruins, and it was a pleasant walk and climb to go up the colorful valley along the red cliff and clamber up and down ladders and in and out of caves. Puye was another of the more civilized places, and if the fever caught, there were many other sites up and down the river, still unworked and waiting to be explored. Of course it was against the law to destroy or take away any finds. I heard of only one such case. Two or three hikers discovered a cave along the Jemez River which contained two very ancient and well-preserved vessels, originally meant for food storage. These were turned over to a museum.

From the passion for exploration it was only a step to the mining mania. Mining offered not only exercise but also the spirit of romance of the Old West. It led from perusal of old mining reports to the study of maps and geological tracts, then to a day's drive to a take-off spot and a sizeable hike to the old mine sites, the chance to pick over old dumps and crawl through old shafts, a pleasant picnic, and the trek home again loaded with specimens to swap or display. On one such trip we climbed to the old copper mine high above Twining in the mountain country north of Taos. The old car line was steeper than any mountain trail and long as well. After pawing through all the dump piles, we brought down bags full of the pretty ore. A metallurgist friend placed it in an empty soup can and produced bona fide copper chunks by the fireside.

Another trip took us to Bland, a defunct but once lucrative gold mine. We climbed the mountain to Albemarle in wonder that the old buckboards could have made the trip over the worn tracks still visible in the rocks. Here, although we found fine amethyst quartz, we mined no gold. Lazarus Gulch was a spot rumored to guarantee "color," so I tagged along on a dry-panning expedition and as a result I do have two or three crumbs of gold along with the memory of gulping dust and shoveling dirt and stumbling in and out of old holes all day. Other trips included a secret expedition for thorium, of which I was supposed to know nothing, and of course many expeditions for turquoise. I regret to record that the turquoise samples of which we were so proud were laughed at when one of our youngsters took them with him to an Indian fiesta to trade with the Navajos.

Los Alamos furnished many examples of what group pressure can accomplish. Often we got things by devious wangling, but oftener by two or three souls calling a mass meeting and getting public opinion behind a project for the community. Such a one was the children's swimming pool. The second summer, after a winter blast with plenty of snow, someone decided it was unthinkable that the young were not learning to swim. It was recognized that the shortage of water would exclude the adults from any such project. Plans were made for a small pool for the children and donations poured in. The next weekend, a bulldozer was borrowed, groups of volunteers dug, concrete was poured, a fence was put up, and in a week the pool was ready, with schedules set up according to age groups and volunteer adult supervision. It was a great success. The next spring everyone was stirred by signs of activity about the pool. A fancy cage was being set up and wired all around the area. Was this also being taken over by the Tech Area? Such things had happened before. The commanding officer was hurt when the accusations sifted through. This was a fence to prevent people from throwing beer bottles into the pool and thereby to save the children from possible cut feet.

For the adults, there was little to intrigue a water enthusiast. There was a small pond at an old ranch nearby which on weekdays was used as a testing station. On Sundays we could go there, but a number of water snakes knew about the place, too. The Rio Grande was dirty, and the lovely Santa Cruz Reservoir thirty-five miles away took considerable gasoline out of our carefully calculated supply. If one went, eight in a car was the minimum patriotic load. The reservoir dried up in August, but from May to July it was a blue jewel set in the midst of bare red desert hills. The greatest danger was to sit inadvertently on a cactus. Many was the two- or three-year-old who had to be plucked.

Fishermen, who abounded at Los Alamos as elsewhere, came to the reservoir hopefully, but more often journeyed up the Rio or to the mountain stream near the Valle Grande. It was a practical thing in the days of meat scarcity and rationing to have a good fisherman in the family. This sport, too, could be combined well with a family picnic, and it furnished many pleasant Sundays to some families.

The bachelor group and those who could trade off their children often went in for mountain climbing. This, I thought, was the dullest sport in the world when I first went to Los Alamos, but after a year I began to be infected with that persistent curiosity about what lies ahead and at the top. Now, when I go back West I want to see more of those mountaintops. Behind us were several peaks above ten thousand feet, which made fine Sunday hikes, and across the valley in the Sangre de Cristo Range the peaks were much higher. Truchas Peak and Wheeler Peak were popular weekend pack trips for the hardy, but Lake Peak was very rewarding to a beginner like myself. It was over twelve thousand feet high, yet since one could drive almost to ten thousand feet, it was only a day's walk and from the summit there was a superlative view. Exquisite alpine flowers carpeted the last slope. Many a scientific secret must have been heard by those ancient mountain peaks, for these hikes were an ideal way for the men to get away from their laboratories on Sundays and yet still be able to discuss their mutual worries.

If you wanted active evening sport, a bout with the square dancers gave it to you. From the beginning of the Project, every other Saturday night saw the dancers gathering. They progressed from a phonograph and one caller to rival callers and a fine accordian. A second group formed later had a more esoteric outlook and a membership list. Both affairs were serious, vigorous, and unusual. Square dancing was one of the few activities which cut through social and intellectual barriers. The Fermis came, escorting their teenage daughter and her Spanish-American girlfriend. The GIs came. The foreign colony came. One of the Englishmen, who arrived in this country with only one pair of shoes and some bedroom slippers, felt he could not risk the shoes so he would turn up in his lusty red carpet slippers and last the evening comfortably.

Saturday nights, the mesa rocked with a number of other dances and parties. Fenced in as we were, our social life was a pipeline through which we let off steam—steam with a collegiate flavor. Large dances, which often turned into binges, were popular. They were rowdy and wet parties, but always pretty innocent fun. Even our style of flirting was adolescent—we never could seem to work up a good scandal. It

Saturday nights, the mesa rocked. . . . Fenced in as we were, our social life was a pipeline through which we let off steam. (Los Alamos Historical Museum)

is hard to understand why our group of mature, serious scientists and their wives behaved in this country club manner, so alien to us. Perhaps it was partly that we were given to self-pity. We were isolated from theaters and nightclubs and all other metropolitan delights. When a party came along, we attacked it with an abandon equal to our fantasies of what we would be doing if we were in New York. That ninety percent of us would have been in some quiet campus town, leading a faculty-tea kind of social existence, was a point we all discreetly forgot.

Many of the large parties were held in the single people's dormitories. They were more like fraternity dances than anything else. Small groups drank and sang and gossiped in the tiny bedrooms while others danced in the social hall. This fine tradition had been initiated by the pioneer group of bachelor physicists and chemists who arrived in March and April of 1943. The original idea had been to repay married friends for courtesies, and in the beginning few of the boys brought dates. Seldom have married women had a bigger or better stag line than we had at those dances!

The dorms were the logical place for big brawls since our tiny GI houses had not been designed to accommodate many guests. This did not nonplus us. We jammed people in for dinner or for cocktails. Often everyone could not be seated, and sometimes there was not even standing room and the party overflowed onto the porch.

A popular place in which to entertain was Edith Warner's Tea Room. This was only twelve miles away, beside the Rio Grande. Despite her isolation, and without benefit of gas or electricity, Miss Warner prepared delicious food in her unusual restaurant. The vegetables were from her own garden, and the bread was homemade, often from home-ground flour. After the mildewed greens of the Commissary, Miss Warner's salads seemed like food for the gods.

Our social life reached some sort of peak when it was officially recognized by the British government. Unsolicited, $500 was given to the British Mission at Los Alamos to throw a party celebrating the success of the atomic bomb. The British were much too well integrated with the rest of us to have a parochial spree. They invited their friends and did all the work themselves in order to stretch the $500 over a giant guest list. The typically English dinner featured pork pie and peach trifle. The entertainment was a pantomime depicting Los Alamos living as it had seemed to foreign eyes. And there on that singular mesa in New Mexico, we raised our glasses of burgundy to toast the King.

The British were much too well integrated with the rest of us to have a parochial spree. They invited their friends and did all the work themselves in order to stretch the $500 over a giant guest list. (Los Alamos Historical Museum)

The [British] entertainment was a pantomime depicting Los Alamos living as it seemed to foreign eyes. (Los Alamos Historical Museum)

Quiet evenings at home, then, were the exception rather than the rule. We must be up and about, on a horse, on a dance floor, visiting friends, exploring the country. Our parties and athletic activities were a healthy escape from the nervous strain of the great Project in which we were involved. Without this release in alcohol and fresh air we would have gone mad. As it was, we had a very good time.

CHARLIE MASTERS

Charlie Masters taught special classes in typing and Spanish at the Los Alamos school, while her husband, Paul Masters, was the School Superintendent. Having lived in New Mexico most of her life, she could afford a giggle or two at the effect of the "Land of Enchantment" upon people who discover it for the first time.

The Masters moved to Santa Fe in 1946. Paul worked for the New Mexico State Department of Education, and Charlie became a full-time writer. In 1950 she co-authored *Discovering New Mexico* (The Steck Company Press) with Maude Davis Crosno. By 1952 the Masters were in New York City, where Paul was studying public health at Columbia University. In 1953 Charlie won a prize for the best story of the year in *Arizona Quarterly*. She died that same year.

9
GOING NATIVE

Charlie Masters

In New Mexico, where three dramatic cultures have deposited their separate colorful strata of custom, costume, and language, it has always been easy to go native. The Los Alamosanos, for all their much flaunted individualism, could not quite resist the ancient lure of the land. The effect of the American Southwest upon this wildly scrambled miscellany of Hill-dwellers deposited in its midst for two or three years was rather like that of a virulent disease upon any mixed group of people who have all been equally exposed to it.

Some few proved completely immune. They persisted, throughout a long residence, to live isolated lives in a dream world of their own, longing for their home—that home of brick and ivy and flower-spangled grass, the home that was never like this! Somehow I always pictured these people as having emerged, painfully, from perfect jungles of greenery, with slow, primordial movement. The Southwest, to them, was *so* barren.

Others received only a mild nip from the germ and were able to combat it successfully with the healthful memories and habits and tastes stored up in their own bloodstreams. To this group belonged those who were seen at only an occasional Indian fiesta, when it was convenient; who displayed, apologetically, one or two splendid pieces of Indian pottery, given them by their maids, of course; and who visited only the most prominent archeological sites, those publicized by the best-known authorities, naturally. This cautious brood had obviously taken sick only a little because it was the fashionable thing to do. They would effect a speedy recovery, once removed from the source of infection.

117

Then there were those who had it bad. They were struck down, gasping, by the charm of the place and tossed picturesquely, throughout their stay, in a continual delirious fever of appreciation. It was they who trooped about in gay—and grim—disguises compounded of Mexican embroidered blouses, wide fiesta skirts, weighty belts of Navajo silver, jackets woven in the mountain village of Chimayó, and flat-soled, high-topped, deerskin moccasins from Jemez. The impulses of their eclectic culture ranged far and wide to find satisfaction. It was they who spread Navajo rugs on their floors, Chimayó blankets on their couches, Indian paintings on their walls, and black and red pottery on every available projection of their domiciles. It was they who never missed a Spanish-American fiesta or an American Indian dance, be it as remote as the Navajo Sing, the Zuni Shalako, or that potpourri of all things Indian, the Gallup Ceremonial. It was they who showered bewildered relatives back home with enough baskets, rugs, and clay ware to furnish a new wing for the Smithsonian Indigenous Culture Division (had they been of museum quality). It was they who blithely broke down the reserve of the undemonstrative pueblo Indians in record time, joyfully establishing friendships that were fast, at least in one sense. They wrote home ecstatically to their friends of having dined with Felipe—the son of the world-famous potter, you know—or having visited *in the home* of Juan, an *ex-governor* of his pueblo. These enthusiasts were never daunted by the democratic fact that apparently every adult male Indian is, has been, or some day will be the governor of his pueblo. The Indians took all this like the noble redskins that they are. And finally, it was this group, bless them, who changed, temporarily, the entire economy of northern New Mexico with their free-handed spending and their sudden demand of a handicraft people for something like mass production.

Although this was the most fascinating form of the disease, it was not the most serious one. Clearly, these victims of highly susceptible nervous systems would fall prey to and recover from many such attacks in a life of travel and change.

Those who caught the environmental disease in its fatal form were not so voluble. They had the quietness of doom upon them. Indeed, so inconspicuous were these walking cases that we were frequently unaware of their condition until the final symptom manifested itself with startling abruptness: the victim announced with prophetic calm that he had bought or was going to buy a piece of property in New

Mexico. If the former, he was lost irrevocably. If the latter, there was still a chance for him, for some did change their minds after a little soul-searching about the possibility of living without gas stoves and the morning paper. The property in question was invariably of the outdoor genre, showing how completely the great Western tradition had laid them low. Sometimes it was an abandoned cattle ranch with a tumbledown hacienda awaiting the inspired hand. Sometimes it was an unpretentious fishing cabin on a little stream, cozy among tall pines. Or it may have been a few virgin acres where they would build The House—of stone, or adobe, or logs, but never of frame or brick. Yes, these cases will die of the disease. They will die old and healthy, and probably happy, in New Mexico.

There is yet another manifestation of the affliction, which should perhaps be arranged in a footnote under Group One. It often happens that individuals who have done time here most miserably, who have groaningly endured all the agonies of combined exile, imprisonment, and wanton torture, discover after breaking away from God's country at long last that a small and vicious germ has crept into their luggage and gone with them. Imagine the consternation when one finds that the epidemic so scornfully flouted when one lived near it has reached out infectious fingers to draw one back to his doom! Imagine the chagrin with which these unfortunates creep back clandestinely to the Hill, the mortification with which they admit, when discovered, that life at Los Alamos is superior to that in the outside world. Frequently, they attempt to minimize their surrender by raising a great dust storm of bitter complaint—complaint about the shortages, the crowding, the noise, the lack of butter, the unfriendliness, and the seventy-five-cent movies they have encountered in that outer darkness. But the cold fact remains that they are back and have gone native in spite of themselves.

Every soul on the Hill reflected the untensioned and uninhibiting environment at least in superficial ways, if manner of dressing and grooming may be judged superficial. In this realm, the Yankee frontier tradition had the edge over the Indian and the Spanish. The number of blue jeans and lumberjack shirts ordered by this community must have convinced any mail-order spies that the top secret of the war was in the hands of cowboys. Professors who had always fretted under the collar-and-tie tradition of conservative classrooms now cast aside sartorial restraint and puttered happily about in ragged slacks, plaid shirts, and sheep-lined shortcoats. Women long hampered by the hat-and-glove requirements of campus towns now tramped to tea at friends' houses in flat-heeled moccasins, with bandana-wrapped heads, and threw overalled legs blissfully over the arms of GI chairs as they gossiped.

Of course, it would have been too much to ask the ladies to forego the evening dresses they had cherished through all the vicissitudes of a long overland trek or throughout a harassing overseas voyage. At every formal party these dresses—backless or demure, swirling or classic, frilled or sleek—made their triumphant appearance. The year of a gown's creation did not matter in the least, nor did the quality of which it was created, nor the whim of the creator. Here, the long-tailed dress achieved an unprecedented democracy, the tail being its only necessary credential. These parties were loved and faithfully attended, like parties on shipboard. At Los Alamos, too, a little world had broken loose from its moorings and journeyed in a vast, strange sea. The evening dress was, perhaps, our dearest anomaly on the Hill.

The men, however, luxuriating in clothes that were practical and comfortable and, curiously, becoming, refused to match the splendor

At every formal party these dresses—backless or demure, swirling or classic, frilled or sleek—made their triumphant appearance. (Los Alamos Historical Museum)

of their wives after dark. There was no place that a business suit could not and did not go. The appearance of white tie and tails at a party was a phenomenon demanding scientific investigation.

By their clothes we knew them. A woman wearing a hat anywhere on the Hill, particularly on a weekday, boldly announced that she was one of two things: a recent arrival or a passenger heading for the bus into Santa Fe. There were a few persistent hat-and-glove wearers among us, but they didn't last long. The Hill soon broke them, and away they tripped in their hand-printed afternoon frocks, tapping their high-heeled way back to California. High heels, of course, were also suspect (and impossible, anyway, on the rocky paths), but fur coats were quite common and were much worn over slacks and jeans.

Occasionally we had brought home to us the disconcerting truth that the Hill-dweller had a look of his or her own. In addition to the get-up, there was often a non-American look there, especially among the women: a look of shiningly natural skin, straight bobbed hair, unpolished nails, a strong, athletic figure; the look of a fresh creature who had never been initiated into the mysteries of an American beauty salon, who had not spent her adolescent years slumped on a curved spine in an American movie house. Even in Santa Fe, Hill people could be spotted. This is an astonishing thing if you know Santa Fe—that cauldron where hundreds of incredible ingredients boil and bubble but do not melt. One of our members, an intelligent and sensitive woman of the above-described appearance, returned from a shopping tour to Santa Fe in a state of bewilderment just touched with annoyance. A shop girl had been extremely attentive to her, offering, unrequested, to cash a check for her or even to extend credit; she recognized the shopper at once, she said, as a resident of Los Alamos. (The bomb story had just broken in the press.) Just how, the woman wanted to know, had she been so easily associated with the Hill? Her friends wisely refrained from pointing out any of the obvious clues, not even the skiing utility pouch that she was wearing strapped to her shoulder for a shopping bag.

Although scientists have often been called long-hairs, at Los Alamos that phrase was disproved. A few of the professional men sported out-length hirsute adornments, it is true, but even they were forced to yield the palm in matters of coiffure to that most vivid element of Hill society, the Indians. The slow-moving pueblo women with their square, glossy bangs and bulky, yarn-tied chignons and the small, limp-paced men with the dignity of their faces framed in two long, sleek braids were a constant reminder of the continuity of human life on this Southwestern plateau. They had a ponderous, undisturbed quality which made us remember that their kind had endured through tribal wars, drought and famine, Spaniards and slavery, Yankees and machines, and that assuredly they would have no trouble surviving the atomsmashers. Unhurriedly and with the minimum of adaptation, they altered the manner of their living temporarily to serve the Hill as maids and waitresses, as janitors, firemen, and cooks. But no matter what the nature of their work, their native dignity remained unimpaired.

No one who has eaten in the East Cafeteria will ever forget the kindly, patriarchal face of Chief, an ex-pueblo governor, who had substituted a tall, white cap for colored feathers and who stood in the service line pouring soup into thick bowls and handing them across the counter with all the noble solemnity of a cacique handing out judgments.

Indian maid service may not have been ideal, as maid service. I do not intend, however, to speak of the quality of service, but only of the Indian culture we encountered. The atomic wives discovered, in their own home laboratories, that an Indian woman is profoundly, immovably, and eternally an Indian woman.

The first impression most people received of the Indian domestic was hilariously burlesqued in a pantomime skit performed at the farewell party of the British Mission. (Since they were leaving soon, they could tell all fearlessly.) The scene represented the kitchen in the home of a newly arrived English couple. The wife, harassed by many duties, employs a maid to do the housework. There enters, as the maid, a short, stolid figure shapelessly draped in a gaudy blanket from J. C. Penney's $1.98 stock. The figure moves with the pace of a bored snail to the center of the stage and there turns a glum and owlish eye upon the audience. The crowd breaks into shouts of joy, recognizing Otto Frisch, one of the senior scientists of the British Mission. The maid listens expressionlessly to the detailed instructions of the housewife, who then departs in innocent trust. Left alone, the redskin domestic stalks idly but majestically about the room, examining the disorder with an air of deep disdain. Finally, she picks up a dirty dish from the heap, weighs it speculatively in her hand, and flings it to the floor with a resounding crash. Next, she picks up a few more dishes and gingerly wipes their edges on the bottom of the window curtains. Her work is then done. As recompense for her toil, she snitches a bottle from the refrigerator and swigs its contents appreciatively. When the mistress of the house returns, the maid impassively collects her fee and goes out, leaving the lady fuming with impotent rage.

Although this scene was extremely exaggerated, it did perhaps caricature and cornerstone qualities of the Indian as untrained maid: the ageless, unhurried rhythm, the independence of attitude and action, the failure to meet the in-service standards of New (or old) England, the South, the Middle West, the California coast—or where-have-you-lived-before.

Sometimes the well-known stoicism broke down with amazing rapidity and unlooked-for results. One wife, troubled by the glum silence of her maid all during the first day of her employment, urged her at parting in the evening to be quite informal in the house. They were really very friendly folk, she said. The maid departed, wordlessly. The next morning, however, she popped into the house with a broad smile upon her rotund features. "Good morning, Mary," she greeted the astonished mistress of the house. "How is John this morning?" she inquired cheerfully, as the master entered for his breakfast. Later in the day, she was heard practicing the steps of a native ritual dance, with an aluminum pan as a tom-tom. Stuffy formality no longer troubled that household.

On another occasion and in another household, a weary scientist who had spent the previous night in the laboratory was submerged in deathlike slumber at his home in the middle of the afternoon. He was half-awakened by an insistent rapping on his bedroom door but could not rouse himself sufficiently to answer, whereupon the Indian maid entered the room, approached the bed, and shook his shoulder vigorously until his eyes flew open in bloodshot alarm.

"Bobbie, Bobbie!" she cried cheerfully. "I wanted to tell you goodbye. Are you feeling OK? I am through with my work and am leaving for the day."

What Bobbie replied is not on the record.

The picture had a brighter side, of course. While the white strangers from the great outside world and the oldest native residents struggled to establish a domestic rapport, a process of mutual education was going on. The Indians were loyal and honest, and trustworthy with children. They were generous, too, to those who won their confidence. Many a Los Alamos woman is taking back to her home in some far corner of this continent, or of this world, a work of art strange and beautiful and doubtless wholly unsuited to its new environment. It is a piece of New Mexico earth, shaped by bare hands to near perfection (but not complete perfection, for only machines can achieve that), baked in a mud oven, and rubbed with a small stone to a flawless glaze. The bowls made as gifts of love are invariably superior to those made for money. They are also, in fact, more modern—that is, more serviceable in an Anglo-American home. Often they were designed from instructions given by the recipient-to-be, and often they were glazed inside as well as out, sure evidence of careful and loving work.

If the pottery prepared as gifts gained in excellence, the commercial product of the pueblos seemed to suffer from the mass production resulting from the Hill's unprecedented demand. The best potters of San Ildefonso and Santa Clara (the pueblos nearest Los Alamos) fell weeks and even months behind in the filling of orders. A phenomenal amount of black ware was produced, for the Los Alamos folk had an insatiable appetite for these plain, rich bowls, plates, vases, plaques, and candlesticks which would not shout "regional" too loudly when placed next to Wedgwood or pewter back home. It became almost impossible to buy a new piece not sanctioned by the taste of the Hill or to find a potter with the time to make one. It cost me four Sunday visits to San Ildefonso, I recall, to buy a bowl of two-toned brown (or red, as the Indians prefer to call it) which I had rashly promised as a birthday gift.

These visits, I think, were rather typical of any visit to a pueblo. We drove into the big, clean-swept solitude of the plaza late in the afternoon. Onto the emptiness of the square faced the emptiness of the house fronts, bare, expressionless, and seemingly abandoned. The texture of these houses was fine grained and smooth under their recent mud-packs. Everywhere was the utter desolation of unresponsive cleanness. We felt, uneasily, that we had driven into a dead pueblo of history. However, we soon located a sign over a front door, proclaiming that here lives R—, a potter. And at last, a sign of life: a shaggy dog lay stretched across the threshold where the welcome mat should have been. As I approached, he did not stir a hair from his matted, fur-rug relaxation. Then suddenly—so suddenly that I jumped—a little boy appeared. His ambush had been around the corner of the house, I think. He approached noiselessly and stared up at me with dead black eyes set in a dry clay face.

"Does R— live here?" I asked, trying to pretend I had not seen the big sign.

"Yes," he said, and continued to examine me with his lackluster eyes.

"And is she home?"

"No," he said, with finality.

"No?" I asked, with what I hoped was a hopeful inflection.

"No," he said again, in his chatty way.

"Oh," I said.

It seemed a complete impasse, until I had a brilliant inspiration.

"Ah—where is she?" I blurted.

At once I felt that I had committed an indelicacy. But the boy responded with surprising alacrity, and in a positive flow of three consecutive words, that she was at church.

With no warning, a small girl materialized at his side. She looked at me and then at the boy. At once, they began to giggle and push each other in universal child-fashion. I felt infinitely better.

We drove around the village, visiting other potters' homes. At only two of these did we rouse any response. At both of them we were ushered, with great economy of clear syllabically spoken English words, into long, plastered rooms where tables displayed all manner of black pottery. The walls were hung thickly with basket-plaques, watercolors by Indian artists, and portraits of family members, some in native costume, others in the less picturesque garb of Uncle Sam. At each place where we did not find red pottery, it was politely suggested that we try So-and-So's house, which was then pointed out to us. At last we came full circle back to R—'s house. It appeared as deserted as before, but this time my knock brought R— herself to the door, her immense dark eyes serene and friendly under a fringe of black hair and an arc of bright shawl. She asked me to come in.

I stepped over the woolly dog into a large room that was clean and adequately furnished with factory-made beds, tables, and chairs. The room was cheerful with leaping flames in a small, hive-shaped corner fireplace. On the bed, a tiny, wriggling bundle began to squall, and through an inner door slipped the little boy of my previous chat. The woman took up the baby from the bed and nursed it at a generous brown breast while we discussed the bowl I wished to order.

She admitted that she had very few calls for ware of that color anymore and added that most of the potters were working on the Hill several days a week and did not have much time left for work on the pottery. I told her of my urgent need, to meet the birthday occurring the following weekend. She promised to make the bowl and send it up to me by a neighbor who worked as a maid on the Hill.

When neither the neighbor nor the bowl put in an appearance during the week, I returned to the pueblo the following Sunday to inquire the reason. R— greeted me with a vague smile, which had nothing of apology in it. A little wind, she said, had got into the oven while the pot was baking, and a large crack had occurred.

"A little wind?" I said dubiously.

"A little wind," she said, explicitly, and smiled again, vaguely.

I said I would return the following Sunday.

I did drive down a week later, reflecting along the way that the weather had been calm for the past seven days. My knock brought R—, frank-faced and hospitable, to the door. She seemed mildly surprised to see me. There was no pot for me. Because, she told me, a woman had been visiting the pueblo just as the pot was finished and had fallen in love with it.

"That woman wanted to buy the pot very much," said R—, looking at me with frank, shameless eyes.

"I will be back next Sunday," I said firmly.

It was already too late for the birthday, but this game had begun to intrigue me. R—, still mildly surprised, readily agreed to make another pot for me during the coming week. We went through the specifications once more.

The next Sunday, my now-familiar knock brought a shrunken old woman, R—'s mother-in-law, I believe. Her stooped and shawled little figure went ahead of me into the room, entreating me with nods and becks and wrinkle-wreathed smiles to follow. She picked up the usual vociferous bundle from the bed. After some initial fumbling, we soon established a conversational middle ground of mutually sketchy Spanish, and I asked about the bowl. At that, she brightened, nodded, and went shuffling out into another room. I brightened, too. I was determined to take whatever bowl appeared, regardless of its color or its original destination. In a moment, she returned with the materialization of the vision that had haunted me and inspired my travels for four weeks. It was a thing of beauty.

"How much?" I asked.

She held up three fingers, then retrieved them, held up one alone, and cut across it quickly at the middle joint. It was a good bowl for $3.50, and it was just in time for Christmas.

At Chimayó, the famous little Mexican weaving village north of Santa Fe, the local craft suffered in a similar way. Trading posts that had formerly been lined and heaped with colorful rugs now displayed only a dozen or so, all in commonplace patterns. Of course, the wartime shortage of wools and dyes partially accounted for this condition, but many looms were altogether silent while their operators stoked furnaces and shoveled dirt at Los Alamos for good and steady pay. The drab-colored buses from the Hill traveled daily as far east as Chimayó, as far north as San Juan, and as far south as Santa Fe to pick up their loads of workmen for the new artificial town that could not have survived without them.

The going-native process found its inverted image in a sudden urge felt by many people of the Hill to turn back upon their own roots, to revive their own ancestral songs and dances. People gathered here from all parts of America began to recall that the common blood of the pioneer flowed in their veins. They did homage to this heritage by forming enthusiastic folk-dancing groups. Full, calico skirts of the pioneer era began to appear in the wardrobe side by side with the evening dress. On Saturday nights, the rafters of the North Mess Hall rang to the stamping of boots and the vigorous calls of "Do-si, lady, do-si-do!"

Now it was the natives' turn to stare. Probably with the idea of giving the home folks a treat, a group of San Ildefonso Indians who worked on the Hill invited the folk-dancing group to come to the pueblo and dance for them. The suggestion was received with enthusiasm.

The party at the pueblo was in the charge of a leading family's handsome soldier-son and his attractive and modern wife. The largest hall in the village was prepared for the occasion—a long, chilly, adobe building whose broken windows were artistically covered with fine old blankets. From the rafters dangled clusters of colored crepe-paper streamers. The walls were lined with benches, and long before the party began, the benches were lined with pueblo families: the women, solid bulks of fringed blanket, bumpy with babies, and at their sides a tapering file of brown children, happy and shy and quiet. It was remarkably like the waiting spectators at an Indian dance except that here a roof took the place of the day sky. The hall was semi-lighted with lanterns and semi-darkened with their interesting shadows. Two small iron stoves made futile attempts to drive out the cellarlike chill.

Long before the party began, the benches were lined with pueblo families: the women, solid bulks of fringed blanket, bumpy with babies. (Los Alamos Historical Museum)

Across one end of the room, a long table was gradually filling up with an assortment of goodies brought by the village women. A huge coffee pot steamed on the fire. Each woman, as she entered the front door, was balancing on her arm or her head a large, flat basket or tray of eatables. She would walk the length of the room with undisturbed dignity, nodding pleasantly to acquaintances on each side, and deposit her offering on the food table as though it had been a shrine. The palefaces were late in arriving. The young people of the pueblo filled in the waiting time by moving briskly about, getting all in readiness, while their elders sat along the sides of the room patiently—almost apathetically—awaiting the fusion of the cultures.

At length, the Hill people arrived in a body. The drive through the crisp air, the frontier costumes they wore, and their anticipation of fun all combined to give them a gay and noisy vigor, a ruddy Anglo freshness that swept into the quietly waiting hall like the descent of a wagon train upon old Santa Fe. It was the Yankee invasion all over again.

The Yankees had brought weiners and buns and cases of Coca-Cola. The round, brown cherubs of the benches ogled the bottles with watering mouths. The mechanical men from the Hill also had brought along a record player, several dozen feet of electric cord, and even a generator to make it work. But their ingenuity somehow failed. The player would not run. Silently and sympathetically, the Indians watched their visitors' noisy, concerted efforts, their shouted instructions, their frantic dashing about. The Yankees were not to be defeated so easily. They had foreseen the possibility of mechanical failure in this environment and had brought with them guitar and violin players to furnish their music. Soon the caller was installed on a high perch, shouting to all to join hands and circle round.

While their white neighbors from Los Alamos stomped in their cowboy boots and whirled their gaudy skirts in imitation of their ancestors, the pueblo people looked on with an interest lively for them. A particularly high swing of a hem on a flushed and panting white lady do-si-doing it for all she was worth made gentle waves of smiles and giggles ripple along the dark benches. The children stared with bright-eyed child-fascination.

When the set was over, it was the Indians' turn. Into the hall pranced three men, gaudy with paint and feathers and jingling with sleigh bells. Behind them moved demurely three women in black tunics weighted with turquoise jewelry. They performed the Dance of the Braided Belts, an intricate and agile movement for the men, a graceful, acquiescing one for the women.

The governor of the pueblo was introduced. The young soldier-Indian made a short speech in his native tongue and then translated it into English. Everybody applauded wildly.

Then slowly, almost slyly it seemed, the tom-tom began to sound. All alone, the ancient instrument insinuated its voice into the clamor, gradually commanding attention, and swelled to an authoritative tune. All alone, it was playing a rhythm suggestive, not of the plaza and the trodden dirt, but of the ballroom and its gleaming floors. Gradually, the people caught the suggestion. One by one, couples began to file onto the floor. And then there was born a new step—or a hundred new steps, for each couple made its own adaptation to this strange fusion of Amerindian rhythm and European motion. The result was a bit fantastic, a bit moving. The pueblo governor moved out with Miss Warner, an old friend of the pueblo. A scientist-guest asked the pleasure of the young Indian hostess. From then on, interracialism was rampant. A good-neighborly time was had by all.

One by one, couples began to file onto the floor. And then there was born a new step—or a hundred new steps. For each couple made its own adaptations to this strange fusion of Amerindian rhythm and European motion. (Los Alamos Historical Museum)

Later, we ate their food with relish: tamale pie, bread baked in outdoor ovens, wild-plum tarts, sugar cookies, pickles, and coffee served with canned milk. They politely munched our hot dogs and drank our bottled Cokes.

This fiesta-hoedown I like to remember as the climax of our relations with the natives. And what I remember best is neither the dancing nor the food, but the quiet friendliness of the woman who sat next to me on the bench. We talked together with the close and casual air of old acquaintances, and I held her baby while she went to fill her plate. It was R—, whom I had heckled and pursued and outwaited, to get my red bowl.